THE STAR FACTOR

WILLIAM SEIDMAN AND RICHARD GRBAVAC

AMERICAN MANAGEMENT ASSOCIATION

New York • Atlanta • Brussels • Chicago • Mexico City • San Francisco
Shanghai • Tokyo • Toronto • Washington, D.C.

Bulk discounts available. For details visit:
www.amacombooks.org/go/specialsales
Or contact special sales:
Phone: 800-250-5308
E-mail: specialsls@amanet.org
View all the AMACOM titles at: www.amacombooks.org
American Management Association: www.amanet.org

This publication is designed to provide accurate and authoritative information in regard to the subject matter covered. It is sold with the understanding that the publisher is not engaged in rendering legal, accounting, or other professional service. If legal advice or other expert assistance is required, the services of a competent professional person should be sought.

Library of Congress Cataloging-in-Publication Data

Seidman, William Henry.
  The star factor / William Seidman and Richard Grbavac.
    pages cm
  Includes bibliographical references and index.
  ISBN 978-0-8144-3320-1 (hardcover : alk. paper)—
  ISBN 0-8144-3320-0 (hardcover : alk. paper)
  1. Leadership. 2. Executive ability. 3. Executives—Training of. 4. Organizational behavior. 5. Career development. I. Grbavac, Richard. II. Title.
  HD57.7.S444 2014
  658.3'14—dc23
                                                        2013033621

About AMA
American Management Association (www.amanet.org) is a world leader in talent development, advancing the skills of individuals to drive business success. Our mission is to support the goals of individuals and organizations through a complete range of products and services, including classroom and virtual seminars, webcasts, webinars, podcasts, conferences, corporate and government solutions, business books, and research. AMA's approach to improving performance combines experiential learning—learning through doing—with opportunities for ongoing professional growth at every step of one's career journey.

Printing number

10 9 8 7 6 5 4 3 2 1

CONTENTS

INTRODUCTION

"**W**e have a big problem." As consultants, we heard that phrase from clients all the time, but in this particular instance it got us started on the research that led us to the methodology at the heart of this book.

We were sitting across the table from the vice president of engineering for a large semi-conductor manufacturing company. We had been brought in to examine the project management practices being used to develop a critical new product. The project was substantially behind schedule, over budget, and torn apart by conflicts.

The troubles were due to dysfunction in the actual leadership structure. The real leaders of the project—six star performers—were completely overloaded. The other 650 people working on it were waiting for them to make decisions. The company asked us to discover what made these six stars so effective and then transfer that knowledge to others so overall productivity could increase. Top management knew that raising everyone to the level of their star performers would have huge financial benefits.

They also said they really disliked consultants and loved systems and tools. They asked us to create a system that could gather the motivating factors and operational efficiencies of their star performers' expertise and supplement it with software tools that could efficiently transfer the stars' qualities to others.

It took us more than two years to do it, but eventually we developed a system that specified what made these stars so good at what they did. After another five years, we had developed a repeatable, cost-effective system for raising others to their level. This project was the genesis of the development process in this book.

We worked for years with organizations in industries as diverse as fast-food companies, government agencies, insurance companies, and high-technology manufacturers. We studied emerging neuroscience research on learning. We came up with our methodology, which we call Affirmative Leadership, to develop more and better leaders in all parts of an organization and in any country or culture faster than people thought possible. These leaders transform their organizations into high-performing machines and their organizational cultures into astoundingly great places to work.

ABOUT US

We were willing and able to take on this work, because we had been students of leadership. As employees of organizations, then as consultants, we have seen a few great leaders and well-run organizations but far more instances of inadequate leadership and poor management. We have experienced what made some leaders great and others not so great and why some people developed into great leaders while others languished.

For Bill, the serious quest to understand leadership began with his doctoral work at Stanford where he studied the effects of management training on group decision making. As part of his dissertation, he developed a measurement tool that could analyze and categorize a star's attitudes and behaviors down to the single word or action.

Rick began thinking about and studying leadership in order to make sense of how Jantzen, a once great company he loved, declined. He found the dismaying results of weak leadership that consistently missed changes to market conditions and made poor decisions about how to respond to them.

In this book you will learn how to develop a comprehensive Affirmative Leadership program. You will learn how to use the science of "positive deviance" to identify and discover your stars' wisdom. You will see how the neuroscience of motivation creates intense motivation in others to learn that wisdom. You will understand how the neuroscience of learning guides learners into developing sustained leadership skills that make a huge contribution to your organization. Anyone and everyone can and should be an Affirmative Leader regardless of their place on an organizational chart, or in their country or culture. Finally, you will learn how creating an organization rich in Affirmative Leaders changes the organization's culture in ways that produce substantial improvements in morale and financial performance.

The book is structured into two main sections. After a brief overview of the science of Affirmative Leadership methodology in Chapter 1, Chapters 2 to 8 show how to develop an Affirmative Leadership program in any organization. They describe the underlying science and actual techniques used with hundreds of organizations to create Affirmative Leaders. We use many examples from real companies, though we use fictitious names and sometimes even change their industries to preserve confidentiality.

Chapters 9 to 11 provide case studies of programs for executives, first-line managers, and individual contributors. They show the possibilities that developing Affirmative Leadership in many roles in an organization can create and the problems it can solve, such as driving a disruptive cultural change or surviving a bankruptcy.

Chapter 12 is about the bottom line in two senses: the

impact of Affirmative Leadership programs on attitudes and behaviors and the financial results it produces. It shows that nine out of ten people in an Affirmative Leadership program demonstrate the attitudes and behaviors of the stars. It also shows how Affirmative Leadership consistently achieves an average return of twenty times the investment. These are results any organization would value.

FOLLOW YOUR STARS TO A BRIGHT FUTURE

UNDERSTANDING THE STEPS TO AFFIRMATIVE LEADERSHIP AND THE SCIENCES BEHIND THEM

QuickBurger was in fourth place in the industry and could not compete with the top three in terms of products or pricing. But Paul, the executive vice president of operations, believed they could outperform the competition. If all of their regional, district, and restaurant managers became as effective in leading their teams as the star performers, QuickBurger could create and sustain a culture of extraordinary guest service that would propel them to first place.

What would it mean to you and your organization if everyone became as good as your star performers? Everyone would be aligned in working toward something important, a compelling collective purpose. Everyone would believe that their teammates had the commitment and skills to achieve it. Organizations filled with this kind of energy are great places for their people and for the bottom line.

This book is about a revolutionary methodology, based on new science and technology that uses an organization's own stars to transform others into extraordinary leaders. Their cumulative impact creates and sustains cultures of greatness. We call this methodology Affirmative Leadership.

Affirmative Leadership is a scientific, proven methodology for creating leadership programs that are based on each company's own unique strengths and needs. Many Fortune 500 companies have used it with astonishing results for their people and bottom line. At one company, employee turnover went from over 250 percent to under 100 percent. An $800 million per year advertising company doubled its sales. A large semiconductor manufacturer's inventory management forecasting became twice as accurate: Each percentage point of improved accuracy increased profits by $50 million.

In the past, because of less than stellar results of previous improvement programs, leaders of organizations have frequently concluded that the risks of driving for significant performance improvements outweighed the benefits. Affirmative Leadership changes the calculus of the risks and makes it easier to commit to change.

This book teaches you how to do what hundreds of our clients have done. Companies who follow the step-by-step process will develop extraordinary organic leadership throughout their organizations. Each step builds on the previous, culminating in both measurable, bottom-line results and a stimulating culture of greatness.

This chapter presents some of the science behind Affirmative Leadership and explains why this new understanding of learning and leadership is important. It then provides an overview of the practical, simple steps for creating affirmative leadership programs that quickly and consistently develop leadership-rich organizations. Ensuing chapters explain the steps in more depth and detail.

THE SCIENCE BEHIND AFFIRMATIVE LEADERSHIP

Affirmative Leadership succeeds where other programs fail because it is based on the synergy between new developments in neuroscience, technology, and the new science of positive deviance (the study of people who dramatically outperform their peers). Affirmative Leadership uses this synergy (Fig-

Affirmative Transformation Model

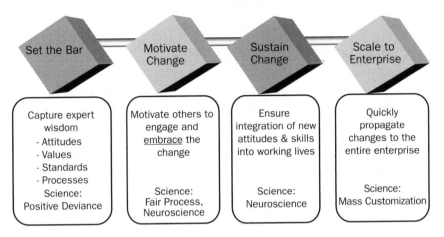

FIGURE 1-1. The science of Affirmative Leadership.

ure 1-1) to inspire and reinforce consistently great leadership from executives, middle managers, team leaders, and individual contributors. It gives organizations both a model for leadership that is particularly effective in the real world of uncertainty and speed and a very efficient methodology for developing more and better leaders.

In traditional approaches to leadership, executives and senior managers set the bar for performance. The science of positive deviance suggests a very different and more effective approach. It says that in any group of people, some consistently and systematically outperform others. These are the stars. Figure 1-2 shows a normal distribution curve of performance with the section on the far right showing positive deviance. The term is from statistics and means a deviation from the average in a desirable direction.

Although "positive deviant" is a well-established technical term that refers to people on this segment of the performance curve, "deviant" has negative connotations and limits the phrase to a statistical comparison of performance. Positive

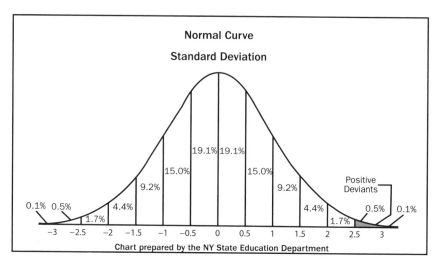

FIGURE 1-2. A normal performance curve.

deviants have a lot more going for them than just being statistically top performers, so we will use the term "positive deviance" when we are referring to the specific body of research but elsewhere in the book we will simply refer to the positive deviants as the "stars"; however, they are a lot more than most people's perceptions of stars.

Stars' attitudes, thinking, and behaviors are different. These people drive the success of your company out of all proportion to their numbers. They love what they do and have a passionate commitment to it. They're not only great at their jobs; they have a profound, compelling sense of purpose that is always aligned with a desire to improve the world for other people. And they get things done. Nothing gets between these people and achieving their mission, whatever the circumstances or situation. They are admired throughout the organization for who they are as much as for what they do. They are your stars: the source of the knowledge, wisdom, and passion the Affirmative Leadership program uses to transform your organization (Figure 1-3).

The next chapters show how to identify the stars and dis-

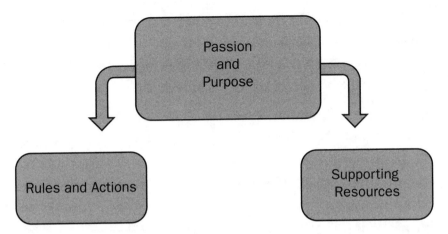

FIGURE 1-3. Star wisdom.

cover their attitudes, thought patterns, and behaviors—the capabilities that make them extraordinary. Readers then learn how to convert their stars' knowledge and attitudes into a written form that is optimized for transfer to others. This becomes a valuable knowledge asset for the organization.

Once the stars' expertise has been correctly documented, readers learn how to use innovative techniques based on the neuroscience of positive images to motivate personnel to engage intensely with this knowledge. The positive techniques stimulate the release of chemicals in the brain that promote enhanced willingness and ability to learn, further motivating people.

This initial enthusiasm is converted into long-term learning, thanks to techniques based on recent advances in neuroscience. Readers see how to develop learning tasks that efficiently drive multiple, positive mental repetitions of a desired new concept or behavior. This leads to long-term internalization of the attitudes and behaviors that boost both morale and performance.

Next, readers learn how to spread the process across the organization, transforming the knowledge as necessary so that it conforms to local needs while maintaining the balance between centralized economies of scale and local empowerment. This has been done successfully even at large, complex organizations, with thousands of leadership candidates spread around the world. New technology, based on mass customization, is what makes it possible.

These new sciences and technologies have changed how we develop leaders and how leaders lead. What was once an ad hoc, inefficient process is now scientific and predictable.

THE AFFIRMATIVE LEADERSHIP METHODOLOGY

Affirmative Leadership is developed and implemented in four phases (Figure 1-4) that have been used in hundreds of companies with tens of thousands of people in all parts of the world with great success. Here is an overview of the phases, including approximately how long each takes, and where in the book each is explained:

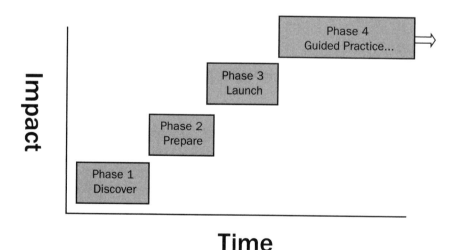

FIGURE 1-4. Four phases of Affirmative Leadership.

Phase 1—Discover: First, a company efficiently and reliably identifies its stars (Chapter 2) and invites them to participate in a three-day workshop designed to help them and the organization discover their wisdom (Chapter 3). A skilled facilitator interviews the group and guides them to define their compelling purpose and articulate how they became so good at what they do.

Phase 2—Prepare: Next, the project team prepares the star wisdom for transfer to others (Chapter 4) by creating a learning program consistent with the neuroscience of learning. This program both optimizes learner motivation and teaches learners exactly how to become like the stars.

The company chooses its coaches (Chapter 4), who will be guiding a learning group of three to fifteen potential Affirmative Leaders through their development program. A facilitator then trains the coaches and guides them through practice coaching for an additional three to four months until they are performing as great coaches.

Phase 3—Launch: Coaches meet with their learning group of potential Affirmative Leaders and begin teaching them. They begin with a six-hour workshop that uses the star wisdom to help the group define a personal and group purpose (Chapter 5) and develop a plan for mastering their roles (Chapter 6). Participants are shown how to become self-directed learners. By the end of the workshop, they are both highly motivated and ready to start an intense learning experience.

Phase 4—Guided practice: For four to six months after the workshop, learners complete weekly practice exercises that require practical application of Affirmative Leadership (Chapter 7). The coaches help each learner adapt and personalize these exercises, lead weekly group discussions about the learning experiences, and systematically drive the reflective learning that leads to internalization of the desired leadership attitudes and behaviors. By the end of the program, more than 90 percent of learners consistently demonstrate the same attitudes and behaviors as the stars.

Everything in Affirmative Leadership can be used with a small group or globally for thousands of leadership candidates at once even if they are in different cultures or countries (Chapter 8). It works the same way every time. When an organization develops Affirmative Leadership in many roles and locations, the organization itself changes, becoming that idealized place to work which we call a "culture of greatness."

Affirmative Leadership is not just for executives: Most companies who have adopted the method have used it to improve performance at all levels, including that of individual contributors. Chapters 9 to 11 are case studies of executives, middle managers, team leaders, and individual contributors learning to be Affirmative Leaders. When all critical roles in an organization are filled with Affirmative Leaders, people's shared purpose and trust in each other's mastery combine to create a superior culture and extraordinary performance.

The results gained through Affirmative Leadership programs are remarkable (Chapter 12). More than 90 percent of the people in an Affirmative Leadership program demonstrate the attitudes and behaviors of the stars. On the financial side, Affirmative Leadership consistently achieves an average return of twenty times the investment.

Affirmative Leadership is so robust and effective that it can develop everyone and anyone in an organization into a great leader. Affirmative Leadership programs have been successfully implemented for customer service representatives in call centers, process technicians on production lines, first-line managers, software programmers, managers, and executives, each of which resulted in significant contributions to the organization's leadership.

THE CALCULUS OF LEADERSHIP DEVELOPMENT

Paul, our vice president at QuickBurger, had studied the costs and benefits of other Affirmative Leadership programs and made a decision to commit to the program at QuickBurger. He weighed all of the data and concluded that Affirmative Leadership was a good investment.

When faced with a need to improve performance, organizations calculate the risks and benefits of committing to a broad-based leadership development program. Because of their past disappointing experiences with traditional approaches to learning and leadership development, they often conclude that the risks of commitment outweigh the benefits.

Affirmative Leadership programs have changed this calculation. The scientific foundation of Affirmative Leadership provides predictable, consistent, low-cost performance improvement. Now organizations can consistently and systematically achieve the performance improvements and the culture of greatness that make an organization a great place to work.

When an organization uses the Affirmative Leadership methodology, everyone makes a significant leadership contribution to the organization's success. Organizations that are bursting with leaders achieve performance levels beyond what people currently can conceive of as possible. It is our hope that you and your organization will follow the steps in this book to achieve those results.

REACH FOR YOUR STARS

FINDING AND UNDERSTANDING YOUR STAR PERFORMERS

Miguel is an architect at Community Construction with a vision about building low-cost schools in declining small towns. When Miguel first showed local people his model for their school, he explained how it could also serve as a community center and library for less money than they had budgeted for the school alone. His passion, energy, and enthusiasm were contagious, and both the school board and townspeople got excited by his vision. The finished school became the true heart of the community, and having such a vibrant center enabled the town to attract and keep good teachers.

When other communities heard about what Miguel had done, they wanted new schools in their towns, too. Again and again, Miguel got the towns' building committees excited about what the schools could do for their communities. The competing construction companies thought they were just bidding on jobs. But because of Miguel, everyone at Community Construction believed they were saving towns—and they were.

Picture the people in your company who are like Miguel—the people who consistently shine at what they do and inspire others. They go by many names: top performers, stars, rainmakers, bright spots, or thoroughbreds. Whatever you call them, these people drive the success of your company out of all proportion to their numbers. They love what they do and have a passionate commitment to it. They're not only great at their jobs; they have a profound sense of purpose and they get things done.

Nothing gets between these people and achieving their mission, whatever the circumstances or situation. They are admired throughout the organization for who they are as much as for what they do. They are your stars and the source of the knowledge, wisdom, and passion the Affirmative Leadership program uses to transform your organization.

This chapter shows what makes stars different and shows you how to begin the process of enabling others to become more like them.

SOCIAL SCIENTISTS AND STARS

Food was scarce in Vietnam after the war; many villagers suffered from malnutrition and even starvation. World food organizations tried and failed to solve the problem, until three social scientists, Richard Pascale and Gerry and Monique Sternin, went to Vietnam to study the situation.

In each village they visited, everyone had access to the same resources, and most people were starving. Yet a few families had healthy, well-nourished children. This, they discovered, was because some women had such a strong sense of purpose that they were willing to do whatever it took to feed their families, including ignoring traditional attitudes about eating. For example, the traditional view was that the shrimp and herbs in the rice paddies were "dirty" foods, so most people didn't eat them. The women whose children were healthy cooked them anyway, so their children got both more food and more protein than the others. Similarly, while most mothers made their children stick to the tradition of eating only at mealtimes, these women let their children snack.

When the researchers figured out what these women were doing, they encouraged them to share their knowledge with others, which dramatically reduced malnutrition in a matter of months. The researchers called the women who managed to feed their families positive deviants, because their performance as mothers deviated positively from that of the rest of the population. Having solved a major social problem by using positive deviants, Pascale and the Sternins extended the idea and studied other populations, such as registered nurses and small business owners. They found positive deviants in whatever group they studied.

Social scientists now know that there are positive deviants—what we call "stars"—in every group, company, and industry. They are the people who consistently and systematically outperform others. They have figured out how to succeed, even in situations or environments others find daunting, and outperform others facing the same issues. What enables them to do this is their attitude to their work. Even when they and those around them can't articulate what this attitude is, it makes a difference to how they think, behave, and are perceived by others.

Miguel, the star at Community Construction, is an example. He couldn't explain what made him different, but he was different and others perceived him as different. He carried himself with confidence, and everyone around him sensed that he knew what he was doing and simply accepted him as an expert. The stars in restaurant chains, federal agencies, insurance companies, women's clothing stores, and every industry have a similar attitude and get the same treatment from others.

Research shows that these people not only behave differently, but actually think differently about their jobs than others do. They have a different mental model, a perspective that makes them more passionate about their work and better at it, too.

Miguel, for example, thinks of each project as a way to revitalize a community, rather than to design another school. His energy and passion are contagious, and people in the community rally around his ideas and build support for them. This creates a collaborative environment in which everyone wins, rather than a builder versus town battle. Because Miguel has a different concept of his job, he approaches things in different ways and achieves different results than his peers.

Many people believe stars are just innately more talented or skilled. Yet stars' thoughts and behavior, whatever their fields, tend to fall into certain very consistent patterns that can be identified and taught to others.

Of these, the stars' passion for what they do is the most important. Their passion for their work determines how they make decisions, hire and train others, perceive risk, and find support.

THINKING AND BEHAVIOR

Stars see themselves as working toward a greater social good, and that makes achieving their goals important, even vital, to them. For example, when asked to describe their jobs at PharMart, star pharmacy managers said, *"I am part of the family emergency response system."* Average pharmacy managers (and PharMart's management, we are sorry to say) said, *"The pharmacy manager's job is to sell 120 prescriptions per day."*

The managers who thought of themselves as helping families consistently sold more than the expected 120 prescriptions a day, while those who saw their role as filling prescriptions didn't. The star passion for purpose drives great results.

This passion for and commitment to achieving a greater social good looks and functions much like what author Dan Pink discusses in *DRiVE*. Pink's extensive research into motivation shows that one of the most important motivating factors is having a higher purpose for your work. This purpose is always about creating a greater social good for others. It is simultaneously far-reaching and humbling, compelling but hard to achieve. The stars' purpose and passion is noticeable, natural, and infectious, and shows up even in industries where you might not expect to see it.

At QuickBurger star managers were passionate about serving their customers—people in a hurry like workers with short lunch breaks or mothers with cars full of hungry kids hurrying to the day's next activity. For these managers, fast service meant giving their guests (they called them "guests," not "customers") a little more time to enjoy their day. Average managers thought of themselves as folks who cook hamburgers and sell them to customers.

Anyone could tell within seconds of entering one of Quick-Burger's restaurants whether a star managed it or not. At the restaurants managed by the stars, the employees welcomed guests with genuine warmth, took pride in what they did, and did it confidently and enthusiastically. The managers' passion and sense of purpose were reflected in their teams' behavior and superior performance.

The stars' sense of purpose also benefits the organization in times of transition. When an organization tries to change its culture, processes, or products, most people resist. Stars see how the changes align with their own purposes and embrace them.

When DigiAd, which sells print ads in yellow pages, started selling Web ads, too, the star sales representatives weren't bothered because they'd never thought of themselves as merely selling ad space. They'd thought of themselves as marketing partners who helped their customers get new business. These reps saw how the Web ads could increase their customers' sales and became very excited about the change. Average salespeople at DigiAd resisted the change, but the stars embraced it and quickly adapted their sales approach to it. You can see the force of stars' purpose in any kind of job, including unexpected ones.

PERFORMING EFFICIENTLY

Stars will not let anything get in the way of achieving their goals. They brush unhelpful comments and procedures aside and carry on. They ignore conventional wisdom when it contradicts their own. Stars focus on the actions that contribute most to achieving their goals.

For example, driven by their desire to give their guests more quality time in their day, the star managers at Quick-Burger outlets emphasized speed of service. They knew that fast service depended on the fryers and drive-through, so during peak business hours they put their best people on the fryers and the next best people on the drive-through. These people not only did things quickly; they felt excited by how quickly they did it, and passed that buzz on to their guests.

By contrast, the average managers at QuickBurger thought of themselves as selling hamburgers. During peak hours they put their best people behind the grill and didn't see how this affected speed of service, nor did they care how it affected customers. If a mother with six kids in the car had to wait longer, who cared?

Stars in all industries instill their purpose in their people, creating a buzz of excitement and greater efficiency. For example, the star managers at PharMart, who felt like they were part of a family emergency response system, hired caring techs who were good at emotionally connecting with customers. They organized inventory and displays so these techs could spend more time with customers. At GetFabulous!, a women's clothes store, the star salespeople think of themselves as helping clients feel confident by having great clothes. They know their customers and what suits them, steer them toward the most flattering choices, and let their best customers unpack clothes when they come in and choose what they want. Everyone has fun and gets excited when they see the new things, and most are bought before they ever reach the racks. In all of these examples, the stars' actions drive productivity in their organizations—as they do in every industry.

USING RESOURCES

Stars take advantage of every opportunity to learn. They review company information, attend trainings, and keep up on industry news. Over time, they become extremely skilled at filtering out what's irrelevant, and focusing on what will improve their performance.

Consider what manufacturing engineers at MegaChip, a large high-technology manufacturing company, said about a three-week training course on how to read the reports generated by one of the company's $50 million machines: *"The course could be taught in three hours if they focused on what accounts for 98 percent of our management issues."* This one piece of advice saved the company three weeks of expensive training time *and* made the course more effective.

Star restaurant managers at QuickBurger dealt just as efficiently with their stack of weekly management reports. For them, food costs, particularly the cost of chicken, were the best indicator of how the restaurant was being managed. If costs and revenues for chicken were in the right ratio, they knew the restaurant was well managed. So out of a report that showed the cost of every item on the QuickBurger's menu by hour, by day, and by week, the stars looked first at the line on chicken. If the chicken numbers were in line with the dollar volume, they knew everything else was fine, too. Star managers reduced a three-inch report to one line.

Stars in all industries focus in on specific high-value information and resources and ignore the rest. At DigiAd, star regional marketing managers knew the best salespeople to include when designing new sales collateral. A hospital emergency department's star case managers knew which social service agencies were best for their patients. This kind of focused knowledge—gained from experience, evaluation, and thought—makes stars better at achieving their own goals and saves their companies significant time and money.

This knowledge comes from lots of hard work. In *Outliers*, Malcolm Gladwell shows that it takes 10,000 hours of work, which is about ten years, to become an expert at something. During this time, developing stars have experiences in a wide variety of related areas, which they then integrate into whatever makes them star performers.

What they learn becomes so much a part of them that they don't even know they know it. They use their knowledge so quickly and naturally that it seems innate—a unique talent or flair—to others. But it isn't. It's compressed knowledge that comes from real experiences, and as such, it can be articulated, analyzed, and converted from unconscious attitudes and behaviors into knowledge and wisdom that are available and teachable to others. You will discover what the stars in your company know by following the process in Chapter 3.

ORGANIZATIONAL CHANGE

When organizations need to change but believe they don't have the expertise to do it successfully, they have three choices. They can hire experts, bring in consultants, or use their own stars. It usually takes new employees a long time to learn enough about their new environment to be effective at changing it. Consultants, too, take time to learn the culture and are often resented and mistrusted by employees. They can be quite expensive, too.

In sharp contrast, a company's own stars are immediately available, inexpensive, culturally aligned, and incredibly knowledgeable. They are admired by everyone and know how to get things done. They are already your go-to people when change is needed.

People are much more likely to embrace an idea, goal,

or change if the organization's stars clarify its purpose and meaning, and then define the actions required to achieve it. This is because the stars do the following:

Earn everyone's admiration. Stars are admired for their past successes and for their abilities to assess and deal with pressing issues. They have so much experience and have been succeeding for so long that they have developed a calm, confident manner that reassures others. When presented with problems, they can usually think of ways to help. When presented with new ideas, they assess them calmly and impartially.

Reflect the best of the culture. Stars embody the organization's values more completely and consistently than most others and this cultural alignment is often more admired and valuable than their expertise. For example, at Mega-Chip, even the top engineers' incomprehensible speech and dorky clothes were admired, because others thought both were signs of being a great engineer. Because people believed the stars' wisdom and knowledge came from their experiences at MegaChip, they were living proof that any engineer who did things the true MegaChip way could become a star with all of the privileges, respect, and rewards. Stars are both role models for and validations of an organization's culture.

Enjoy a reputation for reliability. Because the organization has experienced the stars' consistent success, organizations count on them to be there and perform. This creates tremendous stability for the organization.

YOUR STARS

In Vietnam, identifying stars among the mothers was simple: They were healthy themselves and had healthy children, while everyone else was malnourished and dying. It was a sharp contrast.

MegaChip management thought it would be harder for them to identify their stars, since they had 650 design engineers in 30 countries and 500 customer service people in 5 call centers. But it wasn't. All they had to do was look for the people everyone respected.

In any organization, these are the people everyone respects, as the best in the broadest sense of the word, the ones who consistently and predictably achieve great results in the right way. Everyone in the organization already knows who they are and, if asked the right questions (noted later in this chapter), will name them instantly.

These highly respected people have not only performed consistently; their work benefits others and is completely aligned with the culture's best values. This is why focusing on respect transcends other, more traditional, measures of value. Good metrics alone can be achieved unethically or accidentally. Many intertwined, intangible traits are what really make the difference between someone who is truly extraordinary and someone who is just average or a little above average, and people who are highly respected encompass them all.

Respect also is critical for teaching what the stars know to others. People listen more to those they respect than to those they do not. Research has shown that direction and ideas are much more likely to be accepted from respected peers than from others, because respect minimizes resistance. Thus, the stars identified as a result of the respect question—"Who are the people you most respect for . . .?"—can successfully set the bar for performance in the organization.

When requested to think of a key initiative and asked, *"Who are the people you most respect for their ability to perform some or all of this function?"* every manager in an organization came up with the same list, no matter how large or spread out the organization. For example, QuickBurger had 1,400 restaurant managers; the leadership team named the same 12 managers even though these 12 came from 11 different regions. At AmCo, an insurance company, the leadership team named the same 10 agents even though there were 5,000 agents to consider.

So to find your stars, ask yourself these three questions:

1. Who are the people you most respect for their ability to perform some or all of the functions associated with the initiative, program, or project?
2. Are these the people you would go to if you needed to solve a critical problem or identify leadership for a new initiative, program, or project dealing with this function or area of expertise?
3. If these people told you how to do something would you (a) believe them and (b) do whatever they said to do, without question?

The answer to question one generates a list of probable stars. Questions two and three validate that the people on the list are, in fact, your stars. Just responding to these three simple questions is all you need to do to find your stars.

Many human resource and organizational development specialists, trained in assessments and analytic tools, reject the idea that stars can be identified this quickly and easily. They have often invested a good portion of their lives and egos in doing more formal methodologies and resist this simple approach. To be sure we weren't deluding ourselves about the accuracy of the star list, we used both a more formal analytic process and the three-question approach at the same companies.

For example, when asked to name those they respected most, the management of Community Construction came up with a list of eight people. To test this list, they conducted a more formal statistical analysis of knowledge networks and influence. They got the same eight names plus two newcomers who were not yet well known throughout the organization. Using respect to identify stars works as well in huge global organizations as it does in small local ones.

The more formal analytic method—a variety of network, influence, and knowledge analysis tools —typically took three to four months and thousands of dollars. The three-question approach took minutes and cost nothing. Both methods produced exactly the same lists.

THE VALUE OF STARS

Sometimes leaders of organizations don't think they have any stars. This belief occurs for a variety of reasons. For example, an organization is trying something completely new and doesn't think that anyone in the organization has the relevant knowledge. Or the leaders' paradigm is to trust outside sources, particularly academic sources, more than their own people. Sometimes the leaders just don't think their people are very good. However, every company has some stars, and these people are always critical to improving performance.

Even when a performance improvement initiative is to create something completely new, there may not be anyone who has experience with all aspects of it, but there are always stars in closely related areas. That's why the previously cited questions ask who people respect for "*some* or all aspects of the *new function.*" While there may not be anyone who is highly respected for being expert at all of it, some people are probably respected experts at some aspects of it. If these people work together as a group, a composite portrait of positive deviance in the new role will emerge. This will often include definitions of the new products, services, and/or processes needed for success.

Occasionally—for example, when legal requirements

change—an organization may need outside expertise; but outsiders often cause problems. They rarely understand the culture and thus often speak and act in ways that alienate those within the organization. For instance, Mike, a consultant to MegaChip, found his advice ignored. He never knew it was because his red suspenders and bright bow ties made people think he wasn't a real engineer and therefore couldn't tell them anything valuable.

So when outside knowledge is needed, use your organization's stars as a filter for it. Ask the stars to interpret the expert advice and connect it to their goals and the organization's culture. Using the stars as a bridge between outside experts and internal applicability gives the expertise a much better chance of being useful and accepted.

When a leadership team does not think that any of its people are good enough to be stars, other cultural issues, such as pervasive distrust and anger, are usually prevalent. Even when leaders in these circumstances identify stars, they reject their advice or refuse to act on it. For example, Jim, the vice president of operations for CostLess, a value-priced pharmacy, simply didn't believe that the stars in his organization knew more about local store operations than he did. Cultures that are so deeply dysfunctional that they do not trust their own people are not good candidates for the Affirmative Leadership program.

Your stars are already Affirmative Leaders and, as such, disproportionately drive the success of your company. They hold most of its tribal wisdom and are consistently the most successful and most respected people in it. You can use their sense of purpose—and the esteem in which they are held—to inspire others to learn from them and create a leadership-rich culture.

DISCOVER AND DESCRIBE: THE DETECTIVE

HELPING THE STARS ARTICULATE WHAT MAKES THEM GREAT

GetFabulous! sells "value" women's clothes; Stacy manages their Minneapolis shop, which has topped the chain's sales and profitability lists since she took over. Anyone who walks into her shop senses the energy and excitement; each visitor is made to feel like a special, invited guest. Stacy and her team love clothes and know how to make women look and feel great in them. While Stacy follows most suggestions from headquarters, she's also an innovator and encourages her staff to use their own dress sense to find the best, most flattering clothes for their customers. Stacy and her team produce exceptional results.

If you asked Stacey what makes her so great at her job, she would be hard-pressed to give you an answer. The subtle things that produce outstanding results are so natural to her that she can't explain them. Nor does she really understand why everyone else isn't as successful as she is. Stacey is "unconsciously competent," and her competence combines attitude, knowledge, and skills learned and honed through experience.

Stacy is a star: She consistently and systematically outperforms her peers. Stars organize their thinking in very consistent ways whether they are high-tech design gurus or quick-service restaurant managers. The things they do are so natural to them that they can't understand why others don't

TO FACILITATE A GREAT WISDOM DISCOVERY SESSION

★ Be interested: Have a genuinely inquisitive nature.
★ Capture knowledge in this sequence: Purpose, Big Steps, Principles, Learning Tasks.
★ Ask questions that make participants dig deeper.

automatically do them as well as they do—and they can't articulate what they themselves do, either.

However, it is possible to get the stars to articulate what drives them, and then to explain their knowledge and wisdom so others can learn from them. It is not as easy as just asking them, though. The process, which we call Wisdom Discovery, requires some detective skills to dig beneath the surface and get to the unconscious competence.

This chapter shows how a good facilitator can get stars to articulate and share how they became so successful and what they do to stay that way.

UNCONSCIOUS COMPETENCE

To discover unconscious competence, you must understand the general traits it involves and create an environment in which people can analyze their own attitudes and behavior. Many companies have done interviews to institute best practice implementations and developed nothing more than a list of competencies and to-do lists. Being great at a role entails more than that. If it were as easy as completing a to-do list, almost everyone would be great at their jobs.

Stars, as we saw in Chapter 2, think about their jobs in very different ways and rely on a very compressed set of rules and experiences to make decisions. Interestingly, all stars organize their thinking in fundamentally similar ways. That's why it is possible to use the process in this chapter to obtain a very organized and clear picture of what it means to be great in any role.

The Wisdom Discovery process searches for the following four things from the stars:

- A clear statement of their true purpose in their role (the higher Purpose)
- A big-picture view of the steps or phases necessary to achieve their purpose (the Path to Mastery)
- A deeper definition through principles of what greatness looks like in each of the steps (details of Mastery)
- The activities that build the habits necessary to achieve greatness in the role (Learning Tasks)

These elements, organized and worded according to the latest neuroscience of learning, become the foundation for coaching others to become great in their role.

Facilitating an effective Wisdom Discovery session is very different from facilitating other kinds of meetings and workshops. Guiding stars to dig deep and articulate what makes them different is part art and part science, and experience as a facilitator doesn't always help. We once watched an experienced facilitator fail to capture clients' unconscious competence *and* upset most people in the room by talking too much about his own experiences.

The facilitator's formal title isn't important. The facilitator can be a skilled organizational development process guru, a skilled facilitator from the human resources (HR) department, or a hired workshop leader or trainer from outside the company—anyone who is people-focused and has group management skills. Knowledge of the company or the role being investigated is not necessary or even desirable. Rather, the facilitator needs to understand the different steps in the Discovery process, put his or her own subject matter expertise aside, and listen intently to the stars.

A genuinely inquisitive nature is essential. Someone who's good at Wisdom Discovery has a driving passion to find out why things or processes are important, how things work at the company, where things happen, what the outcomes are, and when things are supposed to happen. A facilitator who asks probing questions with genuine humility and curiosity prompts stars to slow down and think specifically about what makes them great and then articulate that. Then the good facilitator listens intently to the answers and makes sure they get captured.

Too much knowledge of the company or role being investigated, and any kind of bias or ego, prevents this. Ann, for instance, was an excellent general facilitator, but her view of the facilitation process was that she was the expert. Her goal was to lead people to conclusions she had already reached. When she facilitated a Wisdom Discovery, *she* was the star of the process, not the stars. This didn't work. Wisdom Discoveries work only when the facilitator becomes an invisible guide, someone who makes the stars and their expertise the focus.

To find someone who can follow the processes detailed in the rest of this chapter, you may initially need to go outside your company. An outside facilitator brings no bias or preconceived notions to the Wisdom Discovery processes. If you are doing only one Wisdom Discovery, we suggest that you hire someone already trained in the Affirmative Leadership process. If you are doing several Wisdom Discoveries per year, consider training someone on your staff in Affirmative Leadership.

Whoever the facilitator is, the first step is to enroll stars and engage them in the Wisdom Discovery process.

ENGAGING STARS

The facilitator should approach the stars in ways that make them comfortable in sharing their wisdom. Many people believe that stars don't want to give up their secrets for fear that it would somehow diminish them if others in the organization were more like them. Our experience has been that stars are excited to discuss what they do and articulate why they do it.

Our success at enrolling stars has come from following a few basic procedures:

1. Be honest about the reason for needing their help.
2. Point out that their contributions have been numerous and appreciated.
3. Tell them that they will have an opportunity to discuss what it means to be great in their role with a group of their successful peers.

GetFabulous!, a women's value apparel chain with 500 stores, is under constant competitive pressure from the large national chains that have seemingly unlimited advertising and promotional budgets. Their management knows that they must differentiate themselves to stay profitable. Their search for answers shows them that their top-performing store managers are great leaders of their stores' teams, produce the highest sales per square foot, and have the highest employee and customer satisfaction ratings. Betty, the vice president of store operations, says, *"We need all of our store managers to become great leaders like this group."*

The process starts with an invitation to a group of star store managers to attend a Discovery session on how to be a great store manager for GetFabulous!. Betty's invitation includes the importance of learning what they know and how it will affect the organization. The tone of the communication is very straightforward and honest. Rarely are the very best in an organization given a chance to share ideas and discuss best practices with their peers, and stars are always looking for new ideas and new ways to improve their performance.

Diane, one of the Wisdom Discovery participants, for example, immediately sends an e-mail asking *"Who are my peers?"* and goes on to list what greatness means to her. Other Get-Fabulous! store managers, too, become intrigued with this new process of uncovering best practices and are excited to be part of a team of "experts." We find similar responses from invited stars in every organization that we have experienced, throughout the world.

Because this is the first time GetFabulous! has tried anything like Affirmative Leadership, and because she thinks the best store managers will open up more to a stranger than they will with her, Betty decides to hire a trained Affirmative Leadership facilitator to conduct the Wisdom Discovery workshop. She researches Affirmative Leadership facilitators online and finds several people trained in the art of Affirmative Leadership facilitation. With a little due diligence and after speaking with a couple of satisfied former clients, Betty hires Charles to facilitate her Wisdom Discovery.

THE SETUP

Charles's role as facilitator is to ask questions as though he is an intelligent but new store manager, or an average store manager who wants to become a great one. This can be a difficult role for some facilitators. If they are too familiar with the company or role, it is hard to ask naive-sounding questions. However, asking such questions is key to getting star performers to slow down and become introspective enough to articulate their unconscious competence. So the facilitator must be good at both role-playing and asking insightful questions.

The executive sponsor, Betty, kicks off the session by providing context for the program: why we are doing this, how we came to use this approach, and the outcomes we are looking for.

She sets the expectations of the program, why the participants were selected, and how the new process was selected. The facilitator, Charles, then sets the agenda for each of the next three days:

- Day 1: *"This morning we will create a statement which describes your purpose and passion for being a great store manager and in the afternoon we will define the path or steps necessary for others to go through to be as masterful as you."*
- Day 2: *"We will specifically define each of the steps in that Path to Mastery so that others will understand the things they need to learn and know."*
- Day 3: *"We will brainstorm the experiences you had that built your skills as a great store manager over time and link them with any supporting training or materials that you believe to be useful for others. Additionally, you will present the outputs of this three-day session to your management team to show that you have accomplished something valuable here."*

Charles assumes the role of an average store manager eager to become a great store manager. In this role, he is intelligent, competent, and motivated. He just doesn't know how to be great in the job and needs the group to coach *him*.

Some guidelines that Charles provides to assist the stars in their discovery process include:

- Real story: *"Tell me what you need to do your best. There is a difference between the 'official story' and the 'real story.' Here, we want the real story, so tell us what really works. This may make everyone uncomfortable for a little while, but it will become more comfortable soon. Each of you is likely to see 'best' differently, which is great because it will give us insight into what 'best' means. We will come to consensus as we work through this together."*
- Record: *"As you tell me your real story, I record it and project it on a screen. I will record your words very literally—if I don't*

capture the essence of what you mean, please stop me and correct me."

- Slow pace: *"Part of capturing your secret sauce requires all of us to slow down and think. This may make you uncomfortable, but we need to do it this way so we can transfer your expertise to others."*

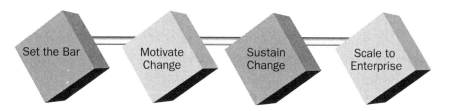

FIGURE 3-1. Affirmative Leadership model.

To help the group of stars understand the overall process, Charles gives them a quick overview of the process of Affirmative Leadership, as presented in Chapter 1, to keep participants focused on the content and formats that are going to optimize the use of their expertise (Figure 3-1).

COMPELLING PURPOSE

The first part of the process is to have the group clearly articulate what drives a great store manager. To create a truly powerful Purpose statement usually takes about four hours of brainstorming, concept gathering, wording, and rewording. Charles is looking for words that evoke an emotional response from others, words that make an average store manager stop and think. We refer to these as power words and phrases. ("Passion" and "excite" are examples of power words.) This Purpose statement must be both concise and specific. If it's too long, people won't remember it. If it's too short or too general, it will lack impact. It also must be in the language of the company and, more importantly, of the stars and their role. Unless it's in that language, those being coached won't relate to the ideas.

Finally, Purpose statements must be true stories: stories really told by stars, not the official stories. Official stories are usually boring and unbelievable. True stories are usually more interesting and believable and, when well phrased, have an obvious sincerity.

Charles asks a simple question to get the discussion going: *"What exactly does it mean to be a* great *store manager?"* The group starts slowly and answers as if they are reading from the company mission statement.

"We sell clothes to women that meet their expectations for fashion and function," says Jenny.

Charles types her response into a document that is projected on a screen in the room.

"We also hire and train associates that learn to help the customers," says Georgette.

"But we also have to handle the financial obligations of the company related to payroll and inventory," says Ed.

Others add their ideas and comments; Charles captures them all and projects them on the big screen. After a few minutes Charles says, *"When I took this job, I was impressed by how much passion and excitement there was. Do you love what you do?"* This question makes the group fidget and sit up a little straighter. *"Does this list of ideas reflect why this job is exciting to you?"*

The energy in the room suddenly changes. People start thinking about why they *love* what they do, not just *what* they do. As Iris says, *"I love the fact that when we have a new product line delivered and we call our 'A' list of great customers, they get so excited about coming into the store to see the new fashions!"*

"To see the faces of our guests and our salespeople when they try on the new lines is the highlight of my day," says Georgette.

The store managers keep talking about how much they love what they do and why, and also how much their jobs mean to them in terms of their higher purposes.

"I love making that special connection with a customer. I can't really describe it, but I know it when it happens," says Toni. Charles keeps recording until there are three or four pages of ideas loaded with powerful expressions of their passion for what they do every day.

After about fifteen minutes of discussion, Charles senses that the energy in the room has slowed; the comments are becoming repetitive, the group is taking longer between comments, and the level of interaction when someone brings up a new idea is less. He says to the group, *"Now we need to consolidate all of these ideas into a single statement of two or three sentences so others understand what it means to be a GREAT store manager. Do that in no more than 300 characters."*

He divides the group into three small teams and tells each that they have an hour and a half to create a statement by highlighting the powerful ideas, then crafting those ideas into a statement no longer than 300 characters.

Why 300 characters? This limitation forces people to boil their thoughts down to the most important and powerful concepts. In its final form, the Purpose statement will be trimmed to around 250 characters. That's because others are going to use it, and the portion of the brain that processes concepts like this can only handle so much information at a time. If the statement is too long, people skim it without processing the important parts. If the statement is too short, there isn't enough there—people can't connect to the ideas in the powerful, emotional way that prompts behavior change. An effec-

TIPS FOR WRITING A GREAT PURPOSE STATEMENT

★ Use power words.
★ Keep the finished statement to about 250 characters.
★ Use the words the participants use.
★ Tell the real story.

tive 250-character statement contains enough power words and emotional content to stimulate thinking, but not enough to hinder it.

After the teams have finished their statements, they present them to the whole group, explaining their reasoning (Table 3-1).

Group 1 focused on creating an atmosphere in which people wanted to work and customers had fun shopping. Group 2 focused on the development of their team to bring about customer satisfaction. Group 3 had elements of both ideas.

Group 1	Group 2	Group 3
I am a great leader of my team. We consistently work to create a fun atmosphere for our customers to shop for their new "look." We think like our customers and our customers are our best advertising.	I lead an energetic group of customer-focused sales associates and our goal is complete customer satisfaction. We provide a fun place to shop and work and try to be an important part of our customers' lives.	I am passionate about developing my people to make an emotional connection with our guests. We create a fun place to shop and work. Our customers look and feel better because of our efforts.

TABLE 3-1. Example of small-group Purpose statements.

Charles explains that they are now going to choose one statement as the foundation and consolidate ideas from the other two into it. The group compares each idea in the other two statements to the selected statement; if any ideas are missing, they add them. This process continues until every powerful idea has been reconsidered and compared. The result is a combined statement that is much too long for anyone to comprehend:

I am a great leader and developer of my sales associates. My energy and passion are infectious and I am an integral part of creating a fun place to work. My team's energy gets our customers excited about looking their best. By being part of our customers' lives, my team makes connections with our customers on a very personal level, which makes it possible for us to fulfill their clothing needs. We help them look and feel their best. Our customers are always satisfied and become our best advocates.

Charles instructs the group to condense the statement to 250 characters. As they do this, the group fine-tunes their ideas into a powerful, concise, and passionate statement.

"I love the part about making an emotional connection. What a great way to think about it!" says Toni.

Jenny adds, *"Our store associates have a cheering session every day before we open just to amp up the energy. No one wants to shop in a blah environment."*

Georgette says, *"I never really thought about becoming part of our customers' lives but we really do! Our customers drop by to tell us when their kids do something great on the soccer field. We are very much part of their lives."*

As the discussion continues, Charles collects the key ideas and re-sorts them into a concise and powerful statement, and again, the group edits it to get the wording just right. This is what the GetFabulous! group produced:

Purpose

As a passionate and energetic leader, I develop my people so they make an emotional connection with all of our customers in a fun and energetic environment. We become part of their lives, which enables us to better fulfill their clothing needs and improve their personal presence.

That's not a typical mission or vision statement. It has a unique, real quality that will resound with others in the same role because it's packed with powerful, passionate ideas and the real reasons great store managers love what they do. It evokes an emotional response—and that is the secret of all effective Purpose statements.

This Purpose statement is the foundation for all that follows. If a new store manager embraces it as her own, she will have a much better understanding of what being great in her role means.

PATH TO MASTERY—THE BIG STEPS

People like to become masterful at things. At work, people often admire those who have achieved great things. They look at those people and think that they could never become that good; but many can, with the right direction and support.

The next step in the Wisdom Discovery process is to define the steps to learning the attitudes, knowledge, skills, and ultimately wisdom to become great at a job. If these steps are defined clearly enough, people can see such a lucid path to Mastery that they believe that they can actually achieve it.

The Path to Mastery is made up of phases, or Big Steps, that present a clear, sequential overall approach to building attitudes, skills, and capabilities. These Big Steps allow those being coached to focus their attention on manageable chunks without being overwhelmed.

There is a limit to the number of Big Steps anyone can process—usually, about six. The portion of the brain responsible for processing and organizing information can adequately hold five plus or minus two concepts at any given time. When the Big Steps are limited to six, people can create a template in their brain for future storage of details.

The steps provide an affirmative picture of the end state, and of what someone will be like at the end of each Big Step. When people have a clear, positive image of where they should be, they have a much better chance of getting there.

Charles tells the GetFabulous! group that they have created a great purpose statement, and then says, *"Now help me get organized to achieve it."* He asks the group to list the steps needed to achieve mastery in their role. His instructions include:

- Create a maximum of six steps or phases.
- The first step is always about vision and values.
- Create a header or title for each Big Step that conveys the key focus and energizes the learner.
- Describe the end result of the Big Step and why it is important.
- Use the first person.

Again, the group is broken into three teams, because multiple perspectives are important. Each team is told to list the Big Steps in becoming a great store manager. Team members think about how *they* learned to make the connections with customers to help them choose their clothes. They then discuss how they teach associates in their stores to become great at those connections. They end by converging on the Big Steps.

When the entire group reconvenes, each team goes through their lists, explaining their thought processes (Table 3-2).

As each team explains their list, the entire group gets new ideas and notices the similarities as well as the significant differences among the lists. Charles now asks what the "right" path for a new store manager is, starting with step 1, "vision and values." As they did before, the group chooses the most powerful statement and works to incorporate powerful ideas from the other two statements.

The facilitator, Charles, now asks many questions to get at specifics:

> *"If you were coaching me to be great in this role, what would you have me working on next?"*
>
> *"If I am great at this Big Step, will I be ready to take on the next step in this process?"*

Big Step	Group 1	Group 2	Group 3
1	VISION: My vision of what I want my store to mean to this community will determine how my people interact with our customers.	MY STAND: Identify the vision of the store— what I want my store to be and what it stands for.	MAKING A DIFFERENCE: I see how we can make a difference in the lives of our customers. We will treat them with respect and help them look and feel great.
2	MY STAFF: I analyze my current staff and project my future needs.	TEAM DEVELOPMENT: I will make sure I have the right people in the right positions to always serve our customers and create a great place to shop.	RUNNING THE BUSINESS: Learning the financial aspects of running a business is key to my development.
3	MY OPERATIONS: Having simple but important operating procedures that are understood by everyone on my staff is crucial for efficient operations.	FINANCES: It is important for me to know all the ins and outs of our financial performance.	DEVELOPING MY TEAM: My employee development and training is crucial for our long-term success.

(continued on page 38)

TABLE 3-2.   Example of small-group Big Steps.

Big Step	Group 1	Group 2	Group 3
4	MY FINANCES: I run a small business and must be fully proficient at understanding the financial implications of my decisions.	OPERATIONAL EXCELLENCE: All of my employees are responsible for operational excellence of the store. The bar is set high and we all strive to achieve it.	PROCEDURES: Effective operating procedures are key to having happy employees and happy customers.
5	MY DEVELOPMENT: Training my team is not a one and done deal. We consistently learn from the visual team and training organization on how to please our customers.	PROCESS IMPROVEMENT: We consistently work to improve all of our work processes by scheduling time for training and learning.	We work together to build a team environment so we can better serve our customers.
6		VISUAL EFFECTS: Visual merchandising is key to our store personality.	CONSISTENT IMPROVEMENT: We create a system to continuously improve our performance over time.

TABLE 3-2. Example of small-group Big Steps.

"What are the most important areas for me to focus on in my development?"

Charles records the responses and helps the group to craft and articulate the key points in a person's development as a great store manager into a single list of six Big Steps (Table 3-3).

Stars create their collective Path to Mastery based on their experience of what it took to become great. It is recorded using

Big Step	
1	MAKING A DIFFERENCE—My store makes a difference in our customers' lives. I make a difference in my team's lives. My vision of what I want my store to stand for in my community drives my daily activities.
2	GROWING PEOPLE—My success is directly linked to my associates' abilities to connect with our customers. I take every opportunity to teach my team how to create value for our customers.
3	OPERATIONAL EXCELLENCE—I execute all the operational aspects of my store consistently and effectively. My customers and associates are more comfortable and satisfied when I make the best operational decisions.
4	ENGAGING MERCHANDISING—A great display tells a story. I create an environment for every associate to tell stories with our merchandise to help create that great connection.
5	FINANCIAL SUCCESS—I fully understand the financial aspects of running a store and all of the implications my actions can produce. I manage my store as if it were my own business.
6	CONTINUOUS IMPROVEMENT—I consistently look for great new talent for our store and the company. My attitude both inside the store and outside helps to attract energetic people to our company.

TABLE 3-3. Example of completed Big Steps.

KEYS TO GREAT BIG STEPS

★ Include six Big Steps at most.
★ Use first person statements such as "I am ..."
★ Focus on the state of what we want to be at the end of the step.
★ Make what we want to be and why very clear.
★ Stay concise.

their particular language and phrasing and is often quite a different path than one might expect. However, steps 2–6 also have some consistent elements. Steps 2–4 usually focus on foundational knowledge necessary to be great such as understanding the product lines, operating models, and building a team of people that align with our Purpose. Step 5 is usually about building support networks both within and outside of the organization. Step 6 is often about expanding the vision and purpose for sustained leadership, including influencing the larger organization.

This list of Big Steps provides a clear, high-level view of the milestones on the way to becoming a great store manager. The Purpose statement and the Big Steps are the foundation for the more specific steps and qualities that are articulated later in the process, and formulating them usually takes all day.

DETAILS OF MASTERY—PRINCIPLES

Too often people are asked to change the way they do things without understanding *what* they are supposed to do and *why* they are supposed to do it. Principles are the stars' articulation of this understanding, gained through years of experience. Before others can follow the Big Steps, they need to understand these Principles. So after listing the Big Steps, the stars articulate their Principles, using the language of the culture. Once people understand the Principles, they can clearly see their path to greatness, understand why they are on it, and fully embrace the Big Steps.

Charles now directs the three small groups to focus on one Big Step each by digging deeper and describing the truly important things for others to know and why they should know it.

The subgroups each work on one Big Step, creating the Principles that are their collective wisdom of what others should know to master that Big Step. This small-group process leads to great discussions about the relative importance of what someone new or average needs to learn to be great. If the discussions take the groups into areas that are nonproductive, the facilitator provides examples of good principles and that quickly gets them back on track.

After the small groups have created their list of up to six principles for their Big Step, the stars reconvene to present their principles to the entire group. Charles drives the discussions to the true core wisdom by asking probing questions and digging deep.

For example, Jerri reads one of her group's Principles: *"We make a difference in our community."*

"Tell me more about how you do this," Charles says.

Jerri's group tells him about fun sidewalk sales, dressing up for Halloween, participating in a local community walk to raise money for cancer research, and providing clothes for a high school fashion show to raise money for the senior prom. Jerri sums it up: *"We live and work in a community and support activities because we can make a difference."*

In the discussion of each principle, Charles captures the powerful ideas and words from the discussion that adds details and nuance to the Principles. He makes sure that the group knows he is capturing *their* words and ideas. Staying true to his naive role, he keeps asking questions that make the group dig deeper. This is because the first time people describe their Principles they tend to leave out the "why it is important to know" part. When Charles leads them into this discussion of the "why," much of the group's wisdom surfaces.

The creation of power-packed Principles makes it much easier to create the learning activities later. Here is an example of Principles for Big Step 1:

MAKING A DIFFERENCE—My store makes a difference in our customers' lives. I make a difference in my team's lives. My vision of what I want my store to stand for in my community drives my daily activities.

- My store will make a difference in this community by creating relationships that go beyond clothes. We conduct all of our interactions with integrity and uphold the values that make this a great store.
- I work diligently to create an energetic, customer-obsessed team that excites each customer, resulting in increased sales and profit. Our team makes this store the preferred place to both shop and work in our community.
- With my manager and my team, I consistently share our progress toward great and achievable goals. We work together to find the way to achieve our goals while making advocates of our customers.
- I own my business and work to align everyone on my team with my vision. I empower my employees to make decisions that further our goals. We live, eat, and breathe our business *every day*.
- I focus my attention on my store and share ideas with my management that might help other stores. My team is constantly working to find new ways to excite our customers.

One of the most important parts of this process is that the star group comes to a consensus that these were the impor-

KEYS TO CREATING GREAT PRINCIPLES

★ Identify the important concepts in the Big Step.
★ Have a maximum of six principles per Big Step.
★ Use the first person and the participants' own words.
★ Focus on the most important things to learn in each Big Step.
★ Make sure the reason for their importance is clear.
★ Stay concise.

tant things to know. They are not just the ideas of one top performer, but represent the collective wisdom of a group of the very best of the organization. The principles are also in the language of the store managers and the organization. For others to truly accept this wisdom as their own, they need to perceive the content as the "real" story and not the "official" story. As one learner later said, *"Whoever put this together really understands my world."*

So creating and refining the principles is worth the entire day it takes. By the end of it, the group has spent two full days thinking about and articulating what it takes to be great in the role of a store manager at GetFabulous!. They have created an overarching vision of the role and the higher purpose of being a great store manager. They have created an organized plan of steps to achieve greatness in the role. And they have defined the things to know and skills necessary to achieve greatness. Next, they identify the experiences and activities that built their attitudes, knowledge, and skills.

LEARNING EXPERIENCES

On day 3, the group lists these experiences and activities. Ideally, the list includes opportunities and experiences that most people in the organization haven't had. These lists are the foundation for the formal learning tasks that will be given to others.

In order to get the small groups focused, Charles says, *"You will now identify the experiences and activities that built your expertise. Go back to the same groups that worked on the principles; but this time, brainstorm everything you can remember that helped you learn the things you know."* Then Charles gives the groups some very specific guidelines:

- First, identify the power words/ideas in the Principle.
- Identify an experience or activity that teaches the concept in the power word.
- Create a preliminary learning task from that experience or activity using words such as observe, present, practice, report, list, attend a class, read, shadow, or interview.
- Just provide a list of ideas. Get us close. We will be rewriting these to conform to the latest neuroscience.

Group 1 brainstormed their list of tasks by first highlighting the powerful ideas in their list of principles for Big Step 1:

- My store will make a difference in this community by creating relationships that go beyond clothes. We conduct all of our interactions with integrity and uphold the values that make this a great store.
- I work diligently to create an energetic, customer-obsessed team that excites each customer, resulting in increased sales and profit. Our team makes this store the preferred place to both shop and work in our community.
- With my manager and my team, I consistently share our progress toward great and achievable goals. We work together to find the way to achieve our goals while making advocates of our customers.
- I own my business and work to align every one on my team with my vision. I empower my employees to make

decisions that further our goals. We live, eat, and breathe our business *every day.*

- I focus my attention on my store and share ideas with my management that might help other stores. My team is constantly working to find new ways to excite our customers.

The first powerful idea is "make a difference in this community by creating relationships." A discussion begins on how they (stars) developed this desire to make a difference in the community.

This led to their first learning activity: Find an inspirational and involved leader and interview them about how they got involved in their community.

As the groups continue to brainstorm activities, Charles prompts them to focus on experiences and activities that will lead people to be *great*, not just good, at what they do. This prompt gets the small groups to dig deeper into the real learning experiences that had helped them become great. These comments came out of the group discussions:

"John Jones is a master at this and is truly inspirational when he talks with groups . . . "

"I remember making a mistake that cost the company a lot of money and June Lamont took me aside and showed me what I could have done differently . . . "

"This book caused me to change my approach to people in this company dramatically . . . "

When the subgroups have described their own learning experiences, they reconvene as a large group and share their lists with the entire group. Here are examples of suggested learning tasks that the stars came up with for Big Step 1:

- Write a vision of what makes a great store.
- Interview/shadow a top-performing store manager.

- Reflect on the idea of integrity and how you can engage your staff in those ideals.
- Write about how your store can make a difference in the community.
- Think about customer obsession and how to build it into your team.
- Find out what other stores (competitive or not) are doing in our area to be special.
- Read a book or article on the power of positive energy in the workplace.
- Be a role model for your staff: Walk the talk.
- Meet with your staff weekly to identify new ideas to be different and to engage customers.

In two-and-a-half days, the group has the foundation of a learning program that includes an impactful Purpose statement, organizational Big Steps that show the Path to Mastery, Principles that clarify why the steps to Mastery are so important, and a raw list of activities that build capabilities. Now, they need to enlist the support of management. There is no better way to garner that support than by having the most respected people in the company share their findings with management.

BUILDING THE COMMUNICATION PRESENTATION FOR MANAGEMENT

While the groups brainstorm tasks, Charles prepares a slide show they can present to management later that day, summarizing the results of the past two-and-a-half days (Figure 3-2).

This presentation is key to the acceptance of the program at various levels in the organization. Initially, it builds support within the star group for their best practices. The better they feel about their efforts, the more they are inclined to talk positively about them. The presentation is a reward—it gives their management a chance to acknowledge and thank them for their efforts. The presentation also demonstrates that the investment of time and money in this project is valuable and will provide tangible results. Lastly, the presentation prompts management to begin thinking about other potential areas on which to use the process.

Having the star group present the outputs of the three-day Wisdom Discovery cements the commitment of the group to the success of the program. It creates a tangible, high-energy buzz in the room that everyone in the room feels. Diane said, *"I was so nervous when I started but it turned out so great!"* The stars' good vibrations are infectious and excite the management team and, later, their colleagues.

This presentation is often the first time many senior managers have ever seen their employees express a practical application of the company's vision. Betty, the vice president

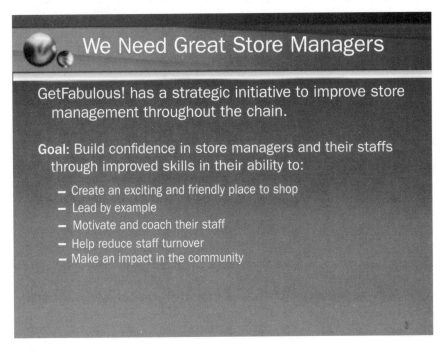

We Need Great Store Managers

GetFabulous! has a strategic initiative to improve store management throughout the chain.

Goal: Build confidence in store managers and their staffs through improved skills in their ability to:

- Create an exciting and friendly place to shop
- Lead by example
- Motivate and coach their staff
- Help reduce staff turnover
- Make an impact in the community

FIGURE 3-2.

of operations who kicked off the GetFabulous! Wisdom Dis-covery session, said, *"This is exactly the program that we need to bridge from our strategic plan to the floor of the stores."*

At most companies, management comes away from the presentation with an elevated confidence that their decision to bring this group of stars together was a good decision. They also gain a better understanding of what it takes to be great in the role. Often it is the first time that they fully understand the power of the star wisdom.

By the end of the presentation to GetFabulous! manage-ment, participants are tired but excited. They are feeling that the workshop is the best three-day development program they have ever been involved in. It is very typical to see the performance of even these star performers improve by 10–20 percent as a result of meeting with their peers in this way. They become advocates for the adoption and utilization of the best practices, which lays the foundation for a successful implementation.

TRANSFORM FOR BRILLIANCE

TURNING THE STARS' WORDS INTO
AN AFFIRMATIVE LEARNING PROGRAM

We were recently in Amsterdam and had an opportunity to visit Coster Diamonds. For 170 years they have been transforming milky raw diamonds into clear brilliant jewels; some of their creations are in royal collections. The company's cutters can examine a jagged rock and envision what it could become. Then they perform the correct cuts to realize their vision and transform the rock into a jewel.

Company transformations also require the ability to see and realize potential. In Affirmative Leadership programs, several different people must have the vision and skill to transform the raw data from the Wisdom Discovery session into learning programs that produce great leaders.

This happens in stages. First, the facilitator and project manager convert the raw learning experiences from the Wisdom Discovery session into engaging learning tasks. This work is based on the latest findings from the neuroscience of learning. Next, the project manager works with management to prepare the measurement systems and tools that will track success. Finally, the facilitator transforms managers into great coaches by showing them how to teach others to embrace the star wisdom as their own. This chapter shows how to make each of these three transformations.

TRANSFORMATION SKILLS

★ **Converting knowledge into learning tasks.** Findings from neuroscience help the facilitator turn the positive deviants' words into engaging learning tasks.

★ **Creating the measurement system.** The optimum approach to measuring the effectiveness of the affirmative leadership program is defined.

★ **Transforming managers into coaches.** Using the expert content, the facilitator models the coaching managers will use on their own teams.

CONVERTING RAW EXPERIENCES INTO EFFECTIVE LEARNING TASKS

Neuroscience has shown that the most effective way to learn and retain what you've learned is a result of short, frequent bursts of mental and physical repetitions of a key attitude, concept, or behavior. Six to eight repetitions of the same idea, over a short period of time, create new neural circuits and new habits. The idea can be repeated in different forms or the same form. While it would work to read the same article six times, we have found it to be most effective to vary the activities by, for example, reading an article, writing something about that article, discussing the article with others, applying something learned from the article to a real situation, writing down what you learned, and telling someone else what you learned. These six repetitions of a single idea would go far in creating long-term learning of it. When this idea is combined with other ideas and activities, the learner begins to create new positive habits.

To create an effective Learning Task the facilitator must:

1. Create Learning Tasks that will help develop the attitudes and behaviors described in the Principles.
2. Design six to eight mental and physical activities that

teach or reinforce the desired attitude, concept, or behavior for each Learning Task. Well-designed activities are short, stimulating, and focused. Their practical value is both obvious and immediate. They encourage learners to reflect systematically and consciously, which leads to deeper and more complete internalization.

At GetFabulous!, Charles begins creating Learning Tasks by reviewing the experiences of the stars. He makes sure that the progressive completion of the Big Steps will accomplish the overall objective of the Purpose statement and that people learning and applying the Principles will be great in their role.

Next, Charles systematically matches the Principles and the Learning Tasks for each Big Step and validates the quality of the repetition stream in each Learning Task. To do this, he begins by creating a chart (Table 4-1) that shows the Principles with power words and phrases in one column and the initial Learning Tasks in another column. In reviewing the columns, Charles is evaluating if the proposed Learning Tasks directly support the power words and phrases in the Principle. He identifies Principles with too many learning tasks, too few, or none at all. From this, he can determine if he needs to refocus the Learning Tasks, thin them, or add new ones. He wants to be sure that there is a Learning Task that teaches every critical idea in every Principle, but nothing extraneous.

He also assesses the quality of each repetition stream. Does each task provide an experience that will drive learning of the Principle? Does the repetition stream begin with something interesting and engaging such as a short exercise, video, or action? Can each task be completed in twenty to thirty minutes? Is it specific (for example, "Write two to three sentences about . . ." versus "Write about . . .")? Does each task clearly apply to real situations? Does each task have five to eight repetitions? If they don't, the facilitator, usually in conjunction with an initiative manager, becomes the stonecutter, trans-

Principles for Big Step 1	Initial Learning Tasks
My store will make a difference in this community by creating relationships that go beyond clothes. We conduct all of our interactions with integrity and uphold the values that make this a great store.	Write a vision of what makes a great store. • Reflect on the idea of integrity and how you can engage your staff in those ideals.
I work diligently to create an energetic, customer-obsessed team that excites each customer, resulting in increased sales and profit. Our team makes this store the preferred place to both shop and work in our community.	• Interview/shadow a top-performing store manager. • Write about how your store can make a difference in the community. • Consider customer obsession and how to build it into your team. • Meet with your staff weekly to identify new ideas to be different and to engage customers.
With my manager and my team, I consistently share our progress toward great and achievable goals. We work together to find the way to achieve our goals while making advocates of our customers.	
I own my business and work to align every one of my team with my vision. I empower my employees to make decisions that further our goals. We live, eat, and breathe our business *every day*.	• Find out what other stores (competitive or not) are doing in our area to be special. • Be a role model for your staff, walk the talk.
I focus my attention on my store and share ideas with my management that might help other stores. My team is constantly working to find new ways to excite our customers.	Read a book or article on the power of positive energy in the workplace.

TABLE 4–1. Mapping experiences to Principles and initial Learning Tasks.

forming the raw ideas of the Principles and initial Learning Tasks into learning diamonds.

At GetFabulous!, Charles asks Betty, the vice president of operations, to help. They begin with the Learning Tasks for the Principles for Big Step 1 and work their way down, deleting some Learning Tasks and enriching others by adding better stimuli (such as online databases and videos that Betty has used in the past) and more repetitions. Knowing that each group will adjust the Learning Tasks to fit specific situations, they make sure the tasks aren't too restrictive. Together, they transform the initial Learning Tasks into a sequence of short, stimulating, engaging exercises that teach the skills and behaviors that Betty wants in her store managers (Table 4-2).

The Learning Tasks provide a structured approach for getting the learner to embrace the desired behaviors. Some Learning Tasks come directly from the experiences of the stars. Some come from what the stars said people needed to know to complete Big Steps. Most are things that they should be doing in their jobs anyway. Doing them with a different mental model (higher Purpose and Principles) makes learners become more like the stars. For example, Betty wants all her store managers and their associates to connect emotionally with their customers. So the Learning Tasks in Big Step 1 contain many repetitions of attitudes, concepts, and behaviors to teach them how to think in those terms, model those behaviors, and then train others to embrace them. Each Learning Task builds on the previous Learning Task to support each Principle. Taken together, they significantly multiply the learning repetitions for each Big Step.

In another example, in a high-tech manufacturing environment, some of the Learning Tasks that resulted from the Wisdom Discovery were to teach Principles that had not been documented before. One of their Principles was about using smells to determine the efficiency of the factory. The stars could determine the "health" of a machine simply by sniffing the air and identifying the odor. So their Learning Tasks included odor identification activities to help new process engineers learn how to do this. By reading the task, setting up their own testing conditions, doing the test, writing about the results, and presenting their results, the engineers performed enough repetitions to create the long-term learning.

Whatever the field, the Learning Tasks are usually short: Each one lasts for, at most, twenty minutes. Reading books takes too long and tends to be too theoretical. Assigning articles and videos (YouTube has incredible resources), or having each person in the group read a chapter and summarize it for the group, is more effective.

Pace also affects the Learning Tasks' impact. Trying to do too many Learning Tasks in too short a period of time, or absorb too much content too fast, overwhelms learners. For example, when a quick-serve restaurant chain attached twenty tasks to five Principles in one Big Step, their restaurant managers lost focus and interest. However, going too slowly doesn't create a strong enough repetition stream to efficiently drive learning. The optimum pace is about two Learning Tasks a week. This is fast enough to keep people's interest but not so fast that learners get overwhelmed. People get mentally tired if a Big Step lasts more than six weeks, so each Big Step is limited to a maximum of six Principles and twelve tasks although eight to ten tasks is better.

The facilitator, Charles, and Betty create a preliminary schedule at the pace of two tasks a week with no more than twelve Learning Tasks per Big Step. At this pace, the store managers will be able to complete the development program in five to six months and won't lose focus within any Big Step.

Charles repeats this transformation process through each Big Step until all the raw material from the Wisdom Discovery is converted to coachable content and optimized to create a great learning experience for others. Performing these tasks in sequence provides hundreds of small, practical repetitions

Principles for Big Step 1	Initial Learning Tasks	Transformed Learning Tasks
My store will make a difference in this community by creating relationships that go beyond clothes. We conduct all of our interactions with integrity and uphold the values that make this a great store.	Write a vision of what makes a great store. • Reflect on the idea of integrity and how you can engage your staff in those ideals.	Read the attached article on vision stories. Write my own vision story for my store and share it with my manager and my associates. View the video on integrity. Write down three powerful ideas from the video and share with my associates.

I work diligently to create an energetic, customer-obsessed team that excites each customer, resulting in increased sales and profit. Our team makes this store the preferred place to both shop and work in our community.	• Interview/shadow a top-performing store manager.
	• Write about how your store can make a difference in the community.
	• Consider customer obsession and how to build it into your team.
	• Meet with your staff weekly to identify new ideas to be different and to engage customers.
		Shadow a top-performing store manager for one day. Log three ideas that I can use for my store and put one into action this week. Journal how the new idea worked and how I can improve on it.
		  In a morning meeting with associates, pose the question: "How can we make a big difference in our community?" Whiteboard the ideas, prioritize them, and have the associates decide how to implement.
		  Create a customer obsession bulletin board and post examples of associates being "obsessed."

(continued on page 56)

TABLE 4-2. Creating good Learning Tasks.

Principles for Big Step 1	Initial Learning Tasks	Transformed Learning Tasks
With my manager and my team, I consistently share our progress toward great and achievable goals. We work together to find the way to achieve our goals while making advocates of our customers.		With my associates, I create a plan to achieve our store goals and plan for monthly reviews with my associates and district manager. Write a short paragraph on the difference between being a satisfied customer and an advocate.
I own my business and work to align every one of my team with my vision. I empower my employees to make decisions that further our goals. We live, eat, and breathe our business *every day*.	• Find out what other stores (competitive or not) are doing in our area to be special. • Be a role model for your staff, walk the talk.	Perform a competitive analysis of stores in the community (see attached form). Report back to associates and generate a list of ideas to become more competitive. Implement one idea.
I focus my attentions on my store and share ideas with my management that might help other stores. My team is constantly working to find new ways to excite our customers.	• Read a book or article on the power of positive energy in the workplace.	Find an article or video on positive energy and share with my associates. Find the two ideas that can impact my store this week.

TABLE 4-2. Creating good Learning Tasks.

of core concepts—the core concepts that make people great in their roles and able to achieve the stars' larger purpose themselves.

MEASURING SUCCESS

Almost every executive at some time asks the question, *"What are my people going to get from this program?"* and uses the answer to determine its fate. Historically, measuring the value and impact of leadership programs has been a significant challenge. Measurement is not an exciting topic for many, but it is essential to establishing the value of the program.

The structure of Affirmative Leadership programs enables easy measurement of the two factors of greatest importance to an organization: attitudes/behaviors (which we call a "demonstration of capability") and business outcomes. The statistics presented earlier about the percentage of people who show the attitudes and behaviors of the stars, as well as the business outcome data, all came from these measurement techniques.

The easiest way to measure behaviors is a confirmation by a "coach" (more on coaches later) who guides a learning experience to make sure that the learner has mastered the key ideas of the Principles and is ready to advance to the next Big Step. For example, by confirming that her store managers have achieved the defined level of performance, Toni, a GetFabulous! coach, controls whether a store manager can advance in the program. Because the coach knows the most about a learner and the confirmation is binary—the learner is confirmed or not—and the accountability for impact is so clear, executives can determine at a glance, often in real time, how effectively a participant is learning and using the stars' expertise. Furthermore, managers and executives can see summaries of progress and recorded learning directly, which gives great insight into the impact of the program.

A more sophisticated way to measure attitudes and behavior is to use a technique we call "certification-lite." In certification-lite the organization surveys a learner's peers, managers, and coach before and after the program by asking the respondent to grade the learner on his or her actual attitudes and behaviors as defined by the Big Step. For instance, a program for first-line supervisors at a major healthcare company that was transitioning into expanded care for elder patients, surveyed the learner's peers, managers, and team to measure the degree to which the first-line supervisor was displaying the attitudes and behaviors required for great Medicare service. The feedback gathered is used to certify that a learner is demonstrating the general attitudes and behaviors of the stars.

A still more sophisticated, but also more demanding technique for measuring a demonstration of capability—formal certification—uses a third party, such as a trainer from another region, to grade students' applications of the Principles through observation or interviews. When done correctly, the rating is statistically valid (it is measuring the correct attitudes and behaviors) and reliable (different people give the identical rating to the same observed capability). However, formal certification programs often raise difficult human resource issues (for example, people who certify as having new and better skills often think they should be paid more), so few organizations use formal certification.

Most organizations also want to assess the impact of Affirmative Leadership on defined business metrics. Creating a correlation between progress through the Big Steps and a good outcome measure is as simple as plotting a line of performance on a chart where the x-axis is progress through the Big Steps. Going further, some organizations have conducted formal pre/post measurements and multiple control groups. For example, one auto parts chain established a baseline for current levels of sales against target and inventory theft before the start of its Affirmative Leadership program and formed two control groups to use as a comparison. They analyzed data on store sales and inventory performance for changes from the baselines and differences from the control groups. While formal measurement provides the best information about the impact of Affirmative Leadership on results, the conditions required for such a controlled measurement program are very rare, so few companies adopt it.

Overall, the multiple possibilities for measurement give organizations an unprecedented ability to monitor and measure their programs. As one executive vice president of a blood products company told us: *"This is the first time I can actually measure the impact of a leadership development program. Now I know what I am getting for my money."*

TRAINING COACHES

It is one thing to have great learnable content and quite another to get people to want to engage with that content. People learn faster and expert content sticks better when they work together in a structured Learning Group led by a trained coach. The coach's job is to guide the group to interact with the stars' content and each other in ways that are consistent with the newest neuroscience of learning. Coaches drive alignment with the Purpose, application of the Principles, adaptation of the Learning Tasks, discussions about the application of the learning experiences, and intense reflection about the learning. Selection and training of the coaches is a key step in transforming transactional environments into transformational cultures of greatness.

Organizations have selected coaches from among their direct managers, volunteer coaches, and nonsupervisory staff and peers (Table 4-3). There are pros and cons to the different selection options.

Direct managers usually make the best coaches because,

Coach Selection	Pro	Con
Direct manager	Improves relationships with staff • Ties manager to the successful development of staff • Aligns priorities between coach and supervisor	Adds perceived additional workload to supervisor • May already believe they are good coaches
Volunteer coaches	• Coaches committed to developing people	• Minimal authority based primarily on personal respect • Difficulty coordinating with the manager
Trainers	• Experienced in facilitation • Usually a primary part of the job function	• Background of telling, not asking • Focus on the "official story" instead of the real story • Difficulty coordinating with the manager
Peers	Grassroots feel to learning	• Minimal authority based solely on personal respect

TABLE 4-3. Pros and cons of coach selection.

at least theoretically, they're already responsible for developing their people and aligning priorities. Coaching Learning Groups should be both natural and already part of their jobs. There are situations in which other coach choices have worked effectively, but our experience is direct managers make the best coaches.

At GetFabulous! with 500 stores spread across 15 states and only a few corporate trainers, Betty's only real option for coaches was to use her district managers (DMs). She expected this to also improve the DMs' leadership skills enough to reduce high turnover, which exit interviews had indicated was due primarily to poor DM support. By making DMs the coaches for their district's store managers, she should be able to directly improve store performance *and* DM skills.

However, few people know how to coach effectively. While some managers have taken formal "coach" training, this isn't often helpful when it comes to teaching deep subject matter and complex skills. This problem is compounded by the fact that most managers believe that they are already good coaches and resist developing their own attitudes, behaviors, and skills in this area. Affirmative Leadership coach training makes a distinction between content coaching and situational coaching. Once resistant managers see the difference, they are receptive to learning content coaching skills.

With Affirmative Leadership, people who have little understanding of coaching and few coaching skills are transformed into great coaches and consistently excellent leaders of group learning.

A five-hour coach kickoff session, called Leading Group Learning, guides the prospective new coaches to examine their ideas about coaching and gets them motivated to learn themselves. Then, it shows them how to coach others and lead structured group discussions on the stars' best practices. Over the next three months, the coaches draw upon the wisdom of other great coaches and practice these skills while actively leading their Learning Groups.

The coach kickoff includes the following elements:

1. Understanding and embracing the higher purpose of being a great content coach
2. Learning the techniques of leading learning groups both in person and in a virtual environment

3. Learning the new science of motivation, fair process, and learning as it relates to coaching expert content
4. Developing communication skills including a great introduction (elevator speech) and the ability to ask provocative questions

Before anyone can develop into a great content coach, they must first understand and embrace the higher purpose of coaching others to greatness. This purpose includes understanding that they need to enjoy helping others develop their skills and become self-directed learners. They need to understand that their role is not to tell people how to be great but to guide people to find how they can become great.

During the Leading Group Learning kickoff session, coaches learn the techniques involved in getting people to embrace expert content: Read/Discuss/Praise/Anchor. They learn how reading aloud helps people comprehend difficult concepts; how adapting content helps the learner personalize the expert content and make it real for them; how praise stimulates brain chemicals enabling both faster learning and reduction of resistance; and how anchoring learning allows long-term habits to form.

Having a basic understanding of the science behind the Affirmative Leadership approach gives the coaches more confidence in their abilities to be a great coach. This session gets the coaches to begin to embrace Fair Process as a basic value and a way of dealing with all people in their lives. When combined with the knowledge of how people think and learn, the results are predictable and positive.

One of the more difficult behaviors to overcome is the urge to tell people the answer to their many questions. Telling people things might be initially faster and easier, but the coaches learn to take the time to ask questions that will enable the learner to think through their issues and come up with the answer on their own. Over the course of several weeks, the coaches use their own learning practicum to build their questioning skills.

THE VALUE OF TRANSFORMATION

There is no shortage of knowledge in the world today, especially in the area of organizational change. The best knowledge comes from your own stars; they already figured out how to be great in your environment. But raw knowledge is a lot like the raw diamond. It requires skills, like those of a diamond cutter, to transform the knowledge of your stars into something that is useful and purposeful.

But having the greatest knowledge in the world has little value if it goes unused. So training people to coach that expert content to others is crucial to the success of your initiative. From call center operations to high-tech manufacturing, from retail to construction, the Affirmative Leadership Leading Group Learning program is now ready to transform ordinary managers and trainers into exceptional leaders.

MOTIVATE THE REST TO BE LIKE THE BEST

PUMPING PEOPLE UP TO EMULATE THE STARS

"More crap from headquarters," said Roger, a pharmacy manager, as he sat, arms crossed, waiting to begin the Affirmative Leadership program. He was sitting with a group of other pharmacy managers who had been selected to move from being good at their jobs to being great at them. Tom, their regional vice president, kicked off the day's session.

"Today we're beginning a journey toward greatness, based on the experiences of top-performing pharmacy managers—respected managers like Gerry Elbert, Sally Reasoned, and Shawn Pone."

The pharmacists all leaned forward, and Roger said, *"Excuse me—did you say this came from Gerry?"*

When Tom said yes, the group settled in their chairs, excited to learn more. Gerry was a star in the organization, and everyone wanted to know how he'd become so successful.

Roger has been dragged through training classes, seminars, weekend retreats, and symposiums so many times that he is now a "functional skeptic"; he does his job and shuts out new ideas. To motivate people like him, you must overcome their immediate resistance by getting their attention and sustaining it, as Tom did when he mentioned someone Roger respected. People learn new attitudes, behaviors, and knowledge faster and use them more when they are highly motivated to better themselves and others.

In this chapter we will show:

- Why most attempts to motivate people fail
- How to use the new sciences of motivation—Fair Process, Motivation 3.0, and the neuroscience of positive visualization
- How to engage and motivate people to learn and to make lasting behavior changes

When the stars' wisdom identified and articulated in Chapter 3—a higher Purpose, the Big Steps of the path to Mastery, the Principles at the heart of those Big Steps, and the Learning Tasks based on the Big Steps and Principles—is presented using the new sciences of motivation (Table 5-1), even the most hardened skeptics embrace the wisdom and change their behavior.

In this chapter and the next, we describe the Launch Workshop, in which the learners build their own personalized Purpose and Learning Tasks. In Chapter 5, we focus on using the new science to help the learners adapt the stars' Purpose, Path to Mastery, and Principles to their needs and priorities. In Chapter 6, we will describe the second half of the Launch Workshop, which is focused on personalizing the specific Learning Tasks. Remember that these Learning Tasks were

Star Wisdom	Sciences of Motivation
Shared higher Purpose	Fair Process
• Path to Mastery (Big Steps)	• Positive visualization
• Principles	• Affirmations
Learning Tasks	• Motivation 3.0
	• Social learning
	Practice, reflection, and journaling

TABLE 5-1.

developed by the coaches (in Chapter 4) based on the stars' learning experiences described in Chapter 3.

By the end of the Launch Workshop, the participants, now motivated and engaged to be self-directed learners, will have developed the specific Learning Tasks that they will apply in the weeks and months following the Launch Workshop, and which will achieve the ultimate goal of Affirmative Leadership: helping all the learners to emulate the stars in their company.

Before we begin with the specifics of the Launch Workshop, however, it's important to understand exactly how the new sciences of motivation overcome resistance to change and learning.

WHY MOST ATTEMPTS TO MOTIVATE WORKERS DON'T WORK

Our understanding of what motivates people has evolved considerably. As the industrial revolution created manufacturing jobs, the motivation was "pay more—get more." Research over the past fifty years has shown that this works only in jobs with limited decision-making. For decision-makers, higher pay alone as an incentive is actually detrimental to performance.

How a proposed change is presented is what counts. Picture Steve, the vice president of a medium-sized manufacturer of sportswear, standing at a podium in a large conference room with his index finger pointing at the audience of manufacturing managers and workers:

"We are going to step into the future by implementing just-in-time manufacturing processes that will improve our ability to manufacture sportswear and reduce our costs. This is going to be the best thing for our company and you as we move this company . . ."

At this point, most of the audience tuned out: They'd just been told what was best for them and their reaction was to stop listening.

They'd also been told that their entire work method was going to change. "Just-in-time manufacturing" means that work-in-process inventories will be reduced and workers will have to learn new jobs to improve the manufacturing times and reduce overall cost. So workers, foremen, supervisors, and management all were upset, to the point of revolution, with this change. They had been a very successful operation and were as efficient a manufacturing operation as there was in the country. As one of them said: *"No way did we need to change, get those marketing geeks to sell differently!"*

THE NEW SCIENCES OF MOTIVATION

What did Steve do wrong? By pointing and lecturing, Steve showed a lack of respect for his people. His words stripped them of power and participation, which made them tune out. Similarly, remember your last performance review. Most of us expect that a significant portion of it will be about what *we* are doing wrong. This creates an intense fight-or-flight reaction and immediate resistance to learning.

We jokingly refer to these situations of "telling" behaviors as "giving people the finger." Most of the time people will return the favor, with a different finger! People don't like being told what to do or what will be good for them. Neurologically, even a benign conversation with a superior can stimulate the amygdala, the part of the brain responsible for fear response, and this often creates an instant rejection reaction to whatever is proposed. Therefore, the mere act of announcing a "great" change to an organization sets up a situation where most people will reject the change!

We now know that one of the best ways to motivate people to accept change is to present that change in ways that increase listeners' dignity and honor. This mind-set, focused on respect for the listeners rather than top-down authority, is known as Fair Process. Fair Process is far more effective than giving people the finger. People listen more and adopt the change more quickly.

Fair Process gathers input and makes decision-making visible. For example, a standard Fair Process approach to changing a manufacturing system might begin with the leadership team meeting with small groups of managers, workers, and foremen to explain the conditions in the marketplace and ask for suggestions. The leadership team would make sure everyone understood that their suggestions would be compared to the suggestions of other groups and considered seriously. Next, the comments would be compiled and presented to all of the employees with a plan based on their suggestions to implement the changes. The employees would set up teams that included workers, foremen, and managers to plan and implement the necessary changes. Notice the collective element at work here. Fair process stresses participation and lots of communication.

This kind of inclusion and transparency exemplifies the Fair Process mind-set. It's important to note that **Fair Process is not a technique, but a way of being, a cultural value.** When a company's leadership truly believes in fair process, receptivity to new ideas and change initiatives increases exponentially. Fair Process is an organization's attitude of respect toward all participants, and it enhances their sense of personal dignity and honor.

MOTIVATION 3.0

The attitude of respect that comes with a Fair Process mind-set becomes even more powerful when it is applied to the meaningful motivators as presented by Dan Pink in his book

DRiVE—Purpose, Mastery, and Autonomy. He calls them Motivation 3.0 to distinguish them from the earlier financial forms of motivation from the industrial age.

The first component of Motivation 3.0 is a sense of Purpose—the social good which gives work meaning. For example, recall at PharMart where average pharmacy managers said they thought of their jobs as *"selling 120 prescriptions per day."* Stars said they thought of themselves as *"a critical part of the family emergency response system."* The stars' Purpose was to create a social good, support for a family in need. Purpose is about creating social value: doing something for others, something that goes well beyond you as an individual. Purpose is what makes some people love to get up in the morning and meet the challenges of the day. Purpose converts a job into a vocation.

The second component of Motivation 3.0 is Mastery. Most people want to be really good at their jobs, particularly when they have a compelling Purpose. However, many people resist striving for a greater Purpose because they don't believe they are good enough and can't see a path to achieving Mastery. For instance, continuing with the pharmacy managers, the stars were incredibly motivated to learn how to provide a great emergency response system because there was such a compelling Purpose that they figured out how to do it.

The average managers, whose Purpose was selling 120 prescriptions a day, were considerably less motivated. When asked if they could become part of the family emergency response system, they said that it *"was a tremendous overreach for our skills."* People will work hard to achieve Mastery only when they have a compelling Purpose *and* believe they can achieve it.

The third component of Motivation 3.0 is Autonomy. People like to have control over their work and their environment; they resent interference from others. Steve's pointing finger and tone told his team he was in control, which stripped people of Autonomy and caused resistance. Being in control is a powerful motivator.

Autonomy or control, however, should not be automatically granted. Instead, and this is true in most organizations, it should be granted only to those who are aligned in Purpose and demonstrate Mastery of their jobs. It is easy to give people autonomy when they are deeply committed to the common Purpose and really good at what they do. For example, a call center was experiencing a high call backlog and many call escalations. After the customer service representatives fully embraced the higher Purpose of "customer centricity in everything I do," and after they'd Mastered the attitudes, behaviors, and knowledge required to be customer-centric, the organization allowed them significantly greater discretion in resolving customer issues. They virtually eliminated call escalations and raised their first call resolutions to 98 percent. Turnover in the group dropped from 90 percent each year to below 5 percent (which is an amazing number for a call center).

In sum, providing people with a great vision of a higher Purpose and showing them the path to become Masterful are key ingredients to creating an autonomous and responsible workforce:

The Fair Process concept explains the power of Motivation 3.0. Fair Process tells us that people want to be treated with dignity and honor. Giving people a higher Purpose, and the skills and knowledge (Mastery) and the autonomy to achieve that purpose, enhances people's dignity and honor.

THE NEUROSCIENCE OF LEARNING

The value of Fair Process and the new sciences of motivation significantly increase when combined with the latest neuroscience research on learning. It shows that positive imagery and written or verbal affirmations cause the release of the neurochemicals that increase openness to new ideas and learning speed. For example, athletes are commonly taught to visualize their success, be it a great golf shot or lacrosse pass, which has been shown to increase performance. David Rock, in his excellent book, *Your Brain at Work,* reports that both positive images and affirmations sharply increase dopamine levels, which are associated with increased openness to new ideas and the ability to learn new attitudes, behaviors, and knowledge faster and more completely.

The stars' collective Purpose statements and Paths to Mastery (see Chapter 3) are among the most powerful positive images for stimulating a desirable neural response. When people envision the tremendous contributions they can make to the greater purpose and visualize their selves mastering a critical attitude, behavior, or body of knowledge, dopamine increases and motivation grows. This new understanding of neurobiology gives better tools for creating change.

Related studies have shown that putting positive images and affirmations in writing transfers neural resources from the portions of the brain associated with fear and resistance to the portions of the brain associated with a sense of control and empowerment (Figure 5-1). The act of writing itself suppresses neural resistance to change and increases openness to change. Furthermore, social learning, such as group discussions and the sharing of the written responses, also has a

FIGURE 5-1. Neural stimulation.

direct neural impact, generating neural chemicals associated with enhanced performance.

Combining the concepts of Fair Process (with its focus on dignity and honor), Motivation 3.0 (purpose, mastery, and autonomy), and the neuroscience of positive imagery, affirmations, and social learning, a substantially new model of motivation has emerged that is scientific, powerful, and effective (Figure 5-2).

The Purpose, Path to Mastery, and Principles from the stars provide an excellent foundation for using all of this new science of motivation. Fair Process is based on communication and interaction rather than one-way directives. Because stars are so respected, others see their wisdom as the best of this collective process. Their definitions are accepted throughout the organization.

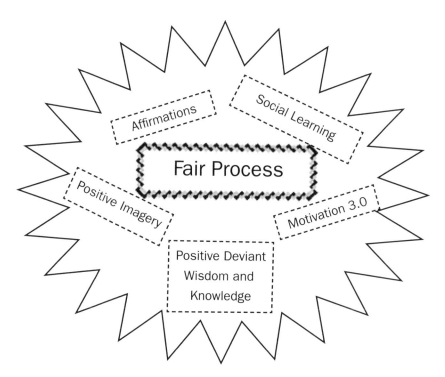

FIGURE 5-2. Affirmative Leadership model of motivation.

The concepts and language of the stars' Purpose, Path to Mastery, and Principles are the foundation for Motivation 3.0 and for using the neuroscience of learning—all three become the basis for the positive images and affirmations and the intense motivation for all learners to become as good as the stars.

READ/DISCUSS/PRAISE/ANCHOR

The new science described earlier led to the Affirmative Leadership Launch Workshop as a powerful methodology for creating intense learner motivation.

In the Launch Workshop, Learning Groups of three to twelve potential Affirmative Leaders are co-led by a coach and an outside facilitator to use the stars' wisdom as a foundation for engagement, intense motivation, and to begin building long-lasting positive habits in organizations.

Before we begin our full description of the Affirmative Leadership Launch Workshop, it's important to discuss the role of the Read/Discuss/Praise/Anchor methodology.

In the Launch Workshop, the facilitator and coaches will guide the Learning Groups to Read/Discuss/Praise/Anchor and thereby reflect on all the elements of the stars' wisdom. Let's start, for example, with the Purpose statement.

Because the positive imagery about the Purpose comes from such respected people, everyone in the Learning Group starts their reflections with positive thoughts. For example, discussing Purpose statements such as *"I make an emotional connection with every customer because . . ."* triggers a positive response. Learners visualize their selves making that connection and see themselves as greater than just their jobs. They start to understand and internalize the higher Purpose presented by the stars, which motivates them to think and perform as they do.

Learners then bring their own experiences to the discussion, which makes the content real to them. It starts to make sense in their situations. For example, a Learning Group of safety consultants was doing Read/Discuss/Praise/Anchor about the meaning and implication of a critical phrase in the Purpose statement about safety leadership— "do no harm." The discussion started with a comment about the Hippocratic oath and the fact that doctors are supposed to adhere to it. This led to a discussion about how they, as safety consultants, act as doctors in the organizations that they serve. They diagnose unsafe situations and prescribe solutions to fix those situations.

One person in the group seamlessly transitioned the discussion from theory to reality by telling how he noticed a seemingly insignificant detail: the size of the safety grating on a cooling fan. While the grating could protect workers from most products, a new smaller gauge product could potentially cause a serious accident. Others in the group related how they had fixed similar issues. They all then wrote down and shared their notions of "do no harm." The star stimulus, realistic discussion, social support, and written anchor enable people to visualize themselves as being as great as the very best.

In very little time, as the store managers and safety consultants in the examples talked about greatness in their own roles, with the obvious implication that they too could be this extraordinary, they experienced the motivational impact of Fair Process. You could see the sense of being personally honored affect them; they sat up straighter, leaned forward, talked with greater intensity, and became emotionally engaged. They also experienced Motivation 3.0 and the neuroscience of positive images and affirmations when they discussed and wrote about the images. Doing both suppressed resistance and encouraged openness. The group process provided social support for creating practical solutions. The result was subconscious acceptance of the star concepts and, after repetition, long-term commitment to the Purpose.

The use of Read/Discuss/Praise/Anchor may seem to be

a simple group discussion of an objective statement, but it's actually a sophisticated methodology for developing intense motivation for a performance improvement.

Read/Discuss/Praise/Anchor are repeated for the Path to Mastery and the Principles defined by the stars. By the end of the Launch Workshop, the learners have a very strong conceptual framework for their Purpose and know how they are going to achieve their Purpose and what Mastery means.

In the remaining sections of this chapter, we are going to describe in detail a typical Launch Workshop based on our GetFabulous! example. The facilitators, coaches, and learners of GetFabulous! will demonstrate the power of the new sciences of motivation and the effectiveness of Read/Discuss/Praise/Anchor as they move through each element of the stars' wisdom:

- Purpose
- Path to Mastery (Big Steps)
- Principles

The Launch Workshop begins, however, with introductions from the coaches. These introductions help set up the respective responsibilities of the coaches and the learners. As the participants quickly realize, Affirmative Leadership is not your typical training program.

INTRODUCING THE AFFIRMATIVE LEADERSHIP LAUNCH WORKSHOP

Charles and Betty planned the Launch Workshop with two DMs coaching their Learning Group of nine store managers each. Each Learning Group gathered around a conference table with their DM and each person's computer. Betty gave a short introduction to set the context. She showed the latest store performance numbers and discussed the competitive nature of the women's apparel business: *"Good is no longer good enough! GetFabulous! is investing in this development program to make sure all our store managers are* great." The store managers sensed that this was not the same old "change initiative of the month" program. Betty was serious and expected them to put in a great effort.

With that, Betty turned the session over to Charles who described the process that they would be going through over the next several hours:

> *"Today is about you planning to be great in your role as store manager. The process is different from other development programs, but it will be fun, engaging, and a great way for you to take control of your own development. Your coaches will now give you a quick introduction of their own before we get started."*

To help the coaches establish their role in the process, Charles had the coaches give the introductions that they'd practiced. The coaches made sure that the group understood that they were guides, not experts—their job was to keep the group progressing toward the goal of greatness. For example, Joan, one of the DMs, introduced herself this way:

> *"I was recently trained in this learning program and, to be completely honest, I had no idea what I was getting into when we started. But as I got familiar with this new way of learning, I became hooked! I think you will love the way we are going to work together to be great in our roles, each learning from the other. I am truly excited to get started!"*

This builds the coach's authority without usurping the group's role, sets the expectations of the group for shared learning, and begins to develop Learning Group cohesiveness.

Some people at her table reacted immediately to Joan's introduction, looking at each other in a peculiar way. They hadn't heard their district manager speak like this before and the idea of learning together was foreign to them. They were accustomed to Joan telling them what they needed to do. As someone on the team said, *"This sounds different!"*

BUILDING MOTIVATION THROUGH COLLECTIVE PURPOSE

It's now time to move to the first element in the learning process: the Purpose statement created by the stars. Remember that the key to getting a group engaged is to use the Fair Process approach and ask questions that spur the Learning Group to think. Thus, each element of the learning process will be read and discussed by the group with their facilitator and coach guiding the discussions. They start with reading on-screen directions that tell them to review the Purpose statement created by the starts and put it in their own words. Charles says, "Be sure to show your passion for this role."

The eighteen store managers are a little tentative in answering; they had not really been paying attention and all had to go back and reread the directions. This is because they were used to training sessions that presented PowerPoint slides, information for them to absorb passively. Doing something to learn was new to them. With this simple question, Charles is telling them that he is not the source of expertise: They will need to act.

One in the group gets it: *"We are going to put their Purpose statement in our own words."*

"Exactly!" says Charles, *"Thank you for your input!"* The person beams just a little from the thank-you. Charles then asks, *"Why do you think it is important to put this in your own words?"*

Someone else answers a little more quickly, *"Because then we will own it."*

Again Charles thanks her for her input and says, *"That is exactly correct! Now notice that the directions ask you to be passionate. Why do you think that your passion is important here?"*

This question prompts the entire group into responses:

"If I am not passionate, who will care?"
"My staff depends on me to bring energy and passion every day."
"Passion is key to me being believable to my customers and my staff."

With these questions, Charles is establishing subtle norms of participation and group learning. While the questions are simple, Charles's use of Fair Process and neuroscience is very purposeful. His questions at the start set the groundwork for how the group will be participating for the rest of the day and throughout the entire Affirmative Leadership program.

His questions make the participants realize that they are expected to attend to the process directions, think about the implications, and apply both to their situations. They are expected to write the Purpose in their own words, be deeply engaged, and show passion. By asking for their reactions, clearly expecting a thoughtful comment typical of a great learner, and praising their responses, Charles honors them. In a matter of a few minutes, the drive to self-directed learning has been initiated.

Next they apply Read/Discuss/Praise/Anchor to the Purpose statement. Charles asks someone to read the Purpose statement aloud, adding, *"As the Purpose statement is being read, the rest of you please think about one powerful idea in this statement that really hits home for you."*

This makes the statement intensely personal, because now it is about something critically important to "you." It also gives everyone in the group responsibility for studying the statement and being ready to discuss what's most important to them.

This time there is no delay. One store manager reads the Purpose statement:

As a passionate and energetic leader, I develop my people so they make an emotional connection with all of our customers in a fun and energetic environment. We become part of their lives, which enables us to better fulfill their clothing needs and improve their personal presence.

"What powerful idea jumped out at you?" Charles asks the first person at the table on his right.

"I like the idea of emotional connection."

"Why did that strike you as important?"

"I never really thought of my role as making connections with customers, but now that I see it, it really is! The better the connection, the better the customer relationship!"

With only two initial directions and two follow-up questions, Charles has driven each person to find an idea that is meaningful to them. The first question makes them really process the statement, to actually think about its powerful ideas. The second question makes them think more deeply about the idea and articulate its importance. Without these questions, most people would scan the statement, nod, and say, *"Got it!"* The questions provoke attention and thoughtful participation.

"Fantastic," says Charles, *"someone else?"*

Now other store managers are listening closely to each other and picking up on most of the key parts of the Purpose statement:

"passionate leader"— *"I have to be passionate in my store. If I'm not, my associates immediately pick up on it and slack off!"*

The group nods in agreement.

"developing people"—*"I know that a huge part of my job is developing my people, but so often we are just scrambling to keep the doors open; our development time goes out the window."*

This comment starts a flurry of responses, some agreeing and some offering how they have made the time.

"fun environment"—*"Sometimes my store has not been a fun place to work, but I can see that having that as one of my overriding goals, I can create that environment and have more fun!"*

Since no one in the group comments on the concept of "personal presence," Charles asks, *"I see that the experts used the words "personal presence" when describing the customer. Why do you think they used those words?"*

Charles uses the stars' knowledge to guide the focus to a powerful idea that stretches the group's thinking. People then move from reacting to the idea to reflecting on the reasons behind the idea's wording, which deepens their understanding of the Purpose.

Everything that Charles does as a facilitator—asking questions, validating answers with praise, asking for other opinions—enhances people's dignity and self-respect. In other words, Charles is putting Fair Process into action. The approach is so significantly different from their prior learning experiences that people quickly become deeply engaged, discussing and sharing their ideas with great intensity and concentration, even when Charles simply asks, *"What jumped out at you?"*

The impact of Charles's questioning is not surprising: About 95 percent or more of those who experience the Fair Process approach engage with the expert content, a far higher success rate than that of most other training approaches.

People are also engaged because of the idea of higher Purpose, which is the first motivator from Motivation 3.0. Every top performer has a higher Purpose for their job. Top Quick-Burger restaurant managers provide a little relief to a soccer mom with a car full of kids. A DigiAd yellow-page salesperson provides new customers for his clients via a combined solution of print and digital options to tell a compelling value story. In order for all employees to be as good as the top performers, they too must embrace a higher Purpose. Higher Purpose is the key to getting people motivated to want to get better at what they do.

Thus, Charles guides the group to develop a personal higher Purpose by driving deeper reflection on being a great store manager. Charles pairs people up to discuss their vision of what that means:

"In your pairs, based on what the stars said about the role of store manager, you have five minutes to talk about your vision of greatness in the role and you have two assignments: learn one thing from the other person and write it down."

Creating the pairs is important because it continues to build on the Fair Process approach. Each person is honored when asked to share his notion of greatness and to teach a peer. Listening to the peer honors the peer, brings new ideas into the discussion, and starts the social support mechanism. Writing ideas down provides legitimacy, generates the neural effects of writing, and drives the transition from the stars' external purpose to an internal, personal Purpose. Two things are going on simultaneously: The group is establishing their own higher Purpose, and they are embracing and internalizing the value of Fair Process.

During the paired discussions, the atmosphere in the room changes. People go from calm and quiet to buzzing with energy and excitement. As everyone describes what it means to be a great store manager, their posture changes; they use hand gestures; their voices rise in pitch. Motivation has soared.

Additional mental repetitions of the Purpose in various forms and groupings further reinforce internalization of the Purpose. Charles changes the pairings and has them repeat the exercise of describing their personal notion of greatness, learning one thing from the other person, and expanding their written notion of greatness. A new dynamic now enters the group. Many of the people reference things they learned in the first pairing and/or what they wrote. The references are usually by name—*"I got this idea from Jo and it is a really good one"*—as they turn their computers so their new partner can see the text.

The second round of pairing provides further support for Fair Process, each person honoring the other person's thinking and for the collective definition of Purpose. Now each individual's definition of their Purpose includes elements provided by a group member. The individual is becoming part of a Learning Group.

Charles then guides the group toward a stronger definition of the collective Purpose and individual ownership of their personal Purpose.

He has the learners gather with their coaches and finish rewriting their Purpose statements, asking them to include all the ideas that they picked up from their fellow learners. The coach asks everyone to share their Purpose statements and asks the team to listen for something that they may have missed:

> *"Plagiarism is entirely OK here! If someone has a great idea that you haven't thought of, add it to your thoughts. We are a team and we are smarter as a group than we are as an individual!"*

As the learners read their statements it is not unusual to hear people say things like, *"I got this from Bill"* and *"I really liked what June said about . . ."*

People are learning from each other and developing a sense of ownership for their own learning. This sense of ownership starts in the very first part of the Launch Workshop when they are asked to edit the Purpose statement, but they don't really notice their ownership until they are finished discussing and writing their own version of the statement. At the end of the Purpose statement discussion, the learners have read and discussed the stars' statement, talked about their notions of greatness, and anchored their own versions of the higher purpose by rewriting the Purpose statement. One participant wrote:

I am a passionate leader of my sales team. My energy fuels my team's attitude every day. (From Jane I learned) To become part of our customer's lives, I must always know them at a personal level. (From Jenni I learned) My customers must feel like we care about the way they look. (From the group discussion I learned) It is crucial that my entire team connects with customers at an emotional level. My customers deserve our best every day.

By now, each member of the group has performed eight or more mental repetitions of the Purpose statement:

1. Heard it read in the whole group
2. Read it again silently
3. Discussed key ideas in the whole group
4. Discussed it again twice in pairing
5. Written it down twice as part of the pairing
6. Discussed it again in the Learning Group
7. Refined the written version
8. Read the written version to the Learning Group

The statement that emerges is a new personalized Purpose statement that includes the ideas from the stars, the individual participant, and the Learning Group.

This Read/Discuss/Praise/Anchor process builds not only personal ownership, but also a group consensus on what greatness means. Everyone in the room is articulating what the same idea means. As their positive energy builds, chemicals are released in their brains that increase their ability to learn and reduce their resistance to new ideas. As a team they are becoming aligned with the higher Purpose of the best people at GetFabulous!. They are starting to pull on the same rope in the same direction.

The key to using this neural foundation of coaching is to get people to:

- Focus on respected expert content that is positive and affirmative in nature
- Discuss that content with a group of peers in an open, accepting environment
- Visualize themselves in those positive terms
- Write down their own visions of greatness, in their own words, to make that vision real for them

SEEING THE PATH TO MASTERY

Each person's Purpose provides reasons for action. As shown in Chapter 4, the Big Steps provide the path to realize the Purpose. A clear, reasonable Path to Mastery defined by highly successful people —the stars—gives learners confidence that the Purpose can be achieved. Breaking the larger Purpose into smaller steps reduces pressure on the portion of the brain responsible for allocating attention, making learning easier, and enhancing long-term retention.

As with the Purpose statement, learners read each of the Big Steps that define the complete Path to Mastery, discuss the key things that they will be learning or doing in those steps, and then anchor their thoughts on why it is important to do those things in writing. Applying Read/Discuss/Praise/Anchor again to the Path to Mastery guides the leader to develop a mental picture of the organization and structure needed to achieve the Purpose. The structure provided by the Big Steps breaks the overall Purpose into smaller, more manageable components.

Returning to GetFabulous!, Charles guides the group to read and discuss the directions that tell people to review the Big Steps and determine the focus and value of the content. He says:

"By discussing each Big Step in the path to Mastery, you are creating a mental template of all of the things you will be learning over the next several months. This is your path to becoming great in your role."

The first Big Step is read aloud:

MAKING A DIFFERENCE—My store makes a difference in our customers' lives. I make a difference in my team's lives. My vision of what I want my store to stand for in my community drives my daily activities.

To get the discussion going, Charles asks a question of the group: *"What do you think we are going to be doing or learning in this Big Step?"*

"Setting our vision?" was the first reply.

Charles nods his approval. To the whole group, Charles poses this provocative question: *"Why do you think setting your vision is important?"*

Various store managers respond:

"If I don't know where I am heading, how can I expect my people to know what to do?"

"Setting my vision is about setting expectations for me and my team."

"I like the idea of setting the expectations."

This gets everyone talking about what they will be doing to make a difference. The noise level in the room rises as more people talk. After just a few minutes, Charles stops the discussion and has everyone finish these two sentences at the end of the first Big Step statement: "My focus is . . ." and "It is important because . . . ." When they are finished, led by their coach, they share their comments with their Learning Group.

This step also uses Fair Process and the neuroscience of learning, but adds a new element: a structure to promote self-directed learning. When people record what they will be learning and why that is important, they become more reflective about the overall learning process. This leads to greater self-awareness and more personal ownership of the learning. Learners then become able to envision a complete program that is substantially more engaging and demanding than a typical training class.

Once the process for guiding the review of the Path to Mastery is established, the coaches lead Learning Group discussions. The participants take turns reading the Big Steps aloud and identifying the main points. Then each group discusses the key ideas and each person anchors them by writing "My focus is . . ." and "It is important because . . ." In about one hour, each person in each group has a clear picture of each of the Big Steps in their Path to achieving Mastery.

Doing this in the smaller groups improves the quality of the discussions, because fewer people in each group means more participation, less fear of sharing ideas, and more bonding. Very subtly, without any overt direction from either the facilitator or the coach, the learning jumps from being somewhat theoretical to highly applied with a practical attitude toward behavior and skill development. The learners start with the Big Step concepts and almost immediately someone says: *"This really is a great concept. Yesterday when I was . . ."* and they go on to describe something that happened to them related to the concept. This creates such powerful engagement and self-directed learning that when several coaches had to leave unexpectedly, the groups continued to work their way through the Big Steps without them. The only problem this intense engagement creates is that it can be too much too fast, so the facilitator and coaches strictly limit the work on each Big Step to twelve minutes.

The learners have now spent about two hours in getting aligned with the stars' Purpose statement, Big Steps, and thinking process. The participants are usually feeling quite good at this point, which creates an opportunity to drive still further the key elements of participation: collective Purpose, Path to Mastery, and self-directed but social learning.

After the Learning Groups have finished Read/Discuss/ Praise/Anchor for all of the Big Steps, Charles leads a group discussion of their role as learners in the learning process. This is a startling idea for many participants. They are rarely asked to reflect on how they learn, but Affirmative Leadership stresses that self-awareness about learning is a funda- mental element of effective leadership.

Charles asks the group for their opinion about the quality and structure of the program: *"Do you think the Big Steps are focusing on the right areas? Do you see anything that is missing or seems inappropriate?"* After some hesitation, mostly because they have never been asked this type of question before, they all say they think the Purpose and Path to Mastery are great.

Charles then asks, *"Who is teaching this program?"*

Invariably they laugh and say they are teaching it; they are teaching and learning from each other.

Charles then says, *"Why is it better for you to teach and learn from each other than from someone outside your Learning Group?"*

Their answers are always something like: *"We live these issues,"* *"We know more about the specifics of our real situation,"* and *"We have so much experience in our group it is really a huge asset."*

"Besides," someone often adds, *"unless someone is really amaz-*

ing, if they are outside our group or organization, we just assume they don't know much so they are never really credible for us." This is often called the "not invented here syndrome," which is a major source of resistance to change. That's why in Affirmative Leadership **everything** is invented here, wherever here is for an organization.

By this point, everyone is laughing and listening closely to Charles. His next question is: *"What is the function of the stars' wisdom?"* Once again, he is guiding the group to reflect on the learning process. Their answer is always something about it being a "starter kit" for their thinking. Finally, he asks: *"What is the role of the system we are following, starting with Purpose and reviewing the Path to Mastery?"* People respond that it guides them to be complete and raises all of the key issues. They also add that this is going to ask a lot of them, but that it certainly is a different and very interesting approach. Charles concludes by telling them they are going to be spending about a month per Big Step reflecting on specific concepts and doing learning exercises.

In most cases, people come into the Launch Workshop thinking it is going to be a typical passive learning environment. Instead, they are working hard on defining their Purpose for being in their role and their path to achieving that Purpose. They are experiencing an amalgam of all of the factors that promote intense motivation and prepare them for active learning. Most of them are ready to actively pursue the learning.

However, a very small percentage of participants, usually less than 5 percent, don't respond to the launch. This occurs for only two reasons. The most common is a condition called "learned helplessness." People who have learned helplessness are experts at getting others to do their work for them, including learning. Since Affirmative Leadership is a highly participatory learning process and these people don't like to participate, they tend to be very resistant to Affirmative Leadership. In the Learning Groups, it is very obvious if someone isn't truly contributing, and the coaches and group tend to put pressure on them to be more active participants. Most people eventually respond to the group pressure and open process and become excellent participants—even (and this happens surprisingly often) the most engaged and active participants.

The other reason people don't respond, and this is less common, is they don't believe in the values presented in the Purpose and Path to Mastery. They reject the values that the most successful people in the organization have defined as the core of success. For instance, in a program that was transitioning software testers to become team leaders, several of the testers rejected the idea that they should assume a leadership role, even though the organization needed them to assume greater responsibilities.

Both kinds of people—the chronically helpless and those rejecting the higher Purpose—will have an adverse effect if left in the Learning Groups. This creates a larger human resources issue. Most organizations do not want to keep people who don't want to work to get better and won't help their teammates. These people often self-select out of the organization, saying things like, *"Now that I know what the expectations for the job really are, I don't want to do it."* Sometimes, they have to be shown the door. Fortunately, though, 95 percent of the people love the Affirmative Leadership Launch Process.

PRINCIPLES: DEFINING GREATNESS IN THE FIRST BIG STEP

Imagine how motivated you would be if you had the opportunity to spend quality time with the top people in your field, the ultra-experts, as they share their deepest and most useful secrets. If you are like most of us, you would be entranced by the discussion, and thrilled to have been able to talk about the ideas with your colleagues. This is the sensation that learners have as they work on the Principles.

Principles are the accumulated wisdom of the stars, the things that the stars know that others need to know to be great in their roles. While Big Steps are the Path to Mastery for achieving the Purpose, Principles are the foundation stones of each step on the Path. Purpose is supported by the Path to Mastery, which is, in turn, supported by Principles. Because Principles are part of a larger conceptual structure, they are easier to review, understand, and internalize. By the time learners work on them, they've been prepared by the Purpose and Path to Mastery and are ready to receive a truly substantive payoff, the specific star wisdom that makes someone extraordinary.

By focusing on the Principles, the Affirmative Leadership Launch Workshop drives greater depth of understanding, commitment, and motivation. The work begins with the Principle beneath the first Big Step. This Principle defines the Purpose more explicitly and expands the vision and values associated with it. Working on the vision and values of the Big Step reinforces motivation. Working on only one Big Step at a time keeps attention directly on the next month's material, which makes it significantly easier for learners to efficiently comprehend the ideas and assimilate the best practices. Later, more Big Steps are added as people demonstrate Mastery of the Principles.

Also, Learning Groups establish stronger interpersonal bonds during the discussion of the Principles, because they're discussing what the stars meant and how the principle applies to real situations. Everyone is interested in the ideas, but even more interested in their application and in helping each other.

Returning to GetFabulous!, Charles guides the group to review the directions for the Principles, which he summarizes: *"Principles are what the stars said everyone needs to know in order to be great in this Big Step. Your job is to discuss the meaning of each Principle and then anchor your ideas by writing these two sentences after the Principle: It means . . . and It is important to me because . . ."*

Here is an example of a Principle in Big Step 1:

Principle 3: I own my business and work to align every one of my team with my vision. I empower my employees to make decisions that further our goals. We live, eat, and breathe our business every day.

These were typical replies:

"I guess I never really thought of the store as my business before. I always felt as if I just worked for GetFabulous!. Owning the store feels different—good, but different."
"If I can get my team to think about it as our store, not some big company's store, I think we can all perform at a different level."
"I already try to empower my employees to make some decisions, but thinking about it in terms of it being our store makes those decisions seem much more real and important."

This is an example of what they typed to anchor their discussion:

This means I will make the decision that is best for my store and my customers. It is important to get this belief through to all of my team members so they can make great decisions too.

The Principles provide the same stimulus that any star would: They get people talking about their values (both personal and professional), ownership, and empowerment. The language itself is provocative and energizing—irresistible to most people. When people think about the Principle's meaning and discuss it with their colleagues, they tend to reflect more deeply and personally about it. The comments are not about the abstract concepts expressed in the Principles but about the speaker's own personalization of them. When they discuss Principles, people talk more about their own experiences, bringing an intensity of focus and engagement that is new to most people's learning experiences. If I put a principle in terms of why it is important to *me*, it becomes my personal affirmation; I embrace it, which reinforces my commitment to the Big Step and the Purpose as well.

By the end of the Principles review, most of the learners experience a startling physiological change. They look more pensive, as though they have already developed significantly greater self-awareness. A common comment is: *"The time passed faster than any class I have ever attended. I feel like I worked really hard, and learned many useful ideas from my Learning Group, the expert knowledge, and my coach. I am looking forward to what comes next."* This reflection and applied learning creates more mental repetitions and leads to faster learning that is sustained.

So in about three hours, people have changed from passive participants to highly motivated learners beginning to drive their own learning experience. They are already showing some of the key attributes of great Affirmative Leaders: self-awareness, a compelling Purpose, an explicit path to Mastery, and a practical definition of greatness.

OPPORTUNITIES CREATED

We were recently talking with the director of talent development for Global Shipping Inc. He said his company had excellent classes and learning tools that never got any traction, because "people just aren't motivated to learn these days." That has not been our experience. After hundreds of launch sessions that included thousands of people, better than nine of ten people get engaged and a meager 2 to 5 percent didn't respond.

OWN YOUR OWN LEARNING

HELPING PEOPLE PERSONALIZE THE LESSONS

When Mark, the coach, left the room to deal with a personal emergency, the group didn't miss a beat. They had just finished discussing "How to Be a Great Client-Centric Account Manager." They had six Learning Tasks left to review, adapt, and schedule. They finished them all then decided to go to a separate room and complete the first task.

When Mark returned later in the afternoon, his group filled him in on what they had accomplished and learned. They didn't need Mark to become efficient learners. They had already become self-directed learners and a self-managing Learning Group.

In this chapter, we finish our discussion of the Launch Workshop. In Chapter 5, we applied the new sciences of motivation to the stars' Purpose, Path to Mastery, and Principles. In the second half of the Launch Workshop, coaches, and facilitators use the new science to help learners adapt the Learning Tasks developed in Chapter 3 and refined in Chapter 4 to their own situations and needs. The end result is a learning plan that they apply in the weeks and months after the Launch Workshop. But the participants will not only have a plan in hand; they also will have been transformed into self-directed learners.

Self-directed learning is directly related to leadership. Because self-directed learners are more proactive and effective at defining and executing their own leadership development programs than passive learners, they are better at becoming great leaders and at dealing with the constantly changing, increasingly complex world. They stay ahead of the many pressures leaders face and model willingness to learn and embrace change for the entire organization. Self-directed learners become great leaders more quickly than passive learners and great leaders are always self-directed learners.

Unfortunately, people in most organizations are passive about their learning. Content has been pushed at them in the classroom, computerized programs, and seminars. When they're pushed, most people resist. It doesn't matter how great the content and presenter are; people block learning when it is force-fed. So most people in organizations become passive learners and need to be taught how to be proactive, self-directed learners. This takes time and practice.

This chapter examines the connection between learning and leading, and the forces that have created passive learners. It describes how Fair Process and the new sciences of learning can help previously passive learners become self-directed learners and leaders. It also teaches self-directed learning and guides the creation of a formal development plan for learning specific leadership attitudes and skills.

KEY LEARNINGS

★ The forces that create passive learners
★ How Fair Process and the new science of learning provide opportunities to develop self-directed learning
★ How to build a personalized learning program designed to achieve the compelling leadership Purpose

LEARNING AND LEADING

"I learn something new every day." This statement by David, the vice president of operations for a global computer company, succinctly expresses one of the more important but least explored aspects of great leadership. David is a great leader because he sees his job as learning about all the new things that hit him and his organization every day. He is consciously and systematically a self-directed learner and, as a leader, models learning for his organization.

Much has been written about the importance and value of having a learning organization, but little of this filtered into the literature on leadership or leadership development programs, even though the concept is supported by noted scientists such as Peter Senge of MIT. In a changing, fast-paced world, leaders who are good at learning and adjusting and are skilled at creating learning cultures tend to prosper while others stagnate and eventually fail. You can't be a great leader without being a great learner, and you can't have a great organization without a culture that values active learning.

For many trainers and other practitioners of leadership development, the notion that the learning process and leadership are this tightly coupled is a novel idea. Yet self-directed learning and leading require many of the same attitudes and skills, as shown in Table 6-1.

Unfortunately, most learners have been socialized into being passive about their development because the structure of the most common learning experiences puts the learner in passive roles with only rare opportunities for engagement. People can cruise through most classes led by instructors or computers without exerting much effort, and nothing more is required of them. The training itself teaches students to be passive learners. While people should, in theory, be proactive about driving their personal development—few people get

Self-Directed Learning	Proactive Leadership
Accepts responsibility for own learning • Understands learning purpose • Adapts learning strategy to maximize value • Efficiently executes learning strategy • Listens to others • Reflects on learning • Is accountable for learning effectiveness • Practices shared Learning • Does scheduling	Accepts responsibility for learning new information • Understands organizational purpose • Adapts organizational strategy to maximize value • Efficiently executes organizational strategy • Listens to others • Reflects on learning • Is accountable for organizational effectiveness • Sets schedules

TABLE 6-1.

up every day and say, "Today I want to be mediocre!"— in the area of learning, that's how most people in organizations behave.

Passive learning is particularly poor for leadership development; yet, paradoxically, most leadership training programs use a passive learning process. Among the most important aspects of being a leader are being proactive, energetic, and taking responsibility for your own and the organization's growth. Passive learning designs and media teach leaders to be passive, just the opposite of the attitudes and behaviors shown by great leaders!

For example, a leadership course designed for managing partners at a large consulting firm included many slides on how to create an exciting mission statement. The materials and presentation were incredibly dull. After the presentation, the managing partners were supposed to craft their own mission statements, but were so anesthetized by the presentation that there was very little energy in the room. The passive structure of the learning design undermined its intent. Passive learning can't teach proactive leadership, nor can passive learning teach realistic leadership. Yet this is just what most leadership development programs try to do, which is one reason they are consistently ineffective.

BECOMING SELF-DIRECTED LEARNERS AND LEADERS

Teaching people to be active, self-directed learners is a critical part of teaching people to be great leaders. One of the primary goals of the second part of the Affirmative Leadership Launch Workshop is to "unfreeze" learners from the passive learning habits and teach people how to be self-directed learners (Figure 6-1). They will be guided to become active learners as they develop personalized learning plans to become great leaders.

To be effective, leadership development has to be applicable and realistic for each individual and situation. It must teach people to think about and lead in messy realities such as handling conflicting agendas and dealing with shortages. Not surprisingly, the best way to create a highly applicable and useful leadership development program is to fully engage the

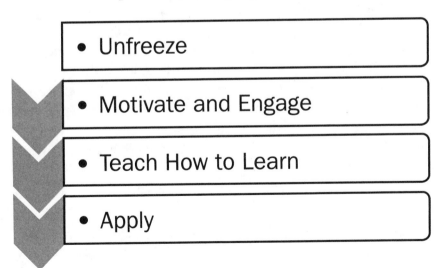

- Unfreeze

- Motivate and Engage

- Teach How to Learn

- Apply

FIGURE 6-1.

potential leader in its definition and execution. When potential leaders develop their own learning programs, the programs fit their unique needs. They are more motivating and more effective. Self-directed learning is not only an essential element in leadership—it is a prerequisite for learning to be a leader.

In order to become self-directed, potential leaders must experience what psychologists call an "unfreeze" that challenges them to reexamine their learning habits, opening them to the possibility of thinking and acting differently. Once unfrozen, people have to want to become self-directed learners and must be taught the attitudes and skills of self-directed learning.

Applying Fair Process specifically to the learning process is a particularly powerful way to unfreeze people from passive learning and motivate the development of the new habits of self-directed learning. By expecting people to be responsible for their own learning, an organization demonstrates a commitment to useful, realistic leadership development while granting the learner considerable autonomy. Both are highly motivating. People are more likely to become self-directed learners when they are allowed to be self-directed. In addition, in treating people this way, the organization is modeling key organizational values about being a learning organization. The learning process is the model for a desired leadership and organizational behavior.

The motivational impact and engagement of applying Fair Process to learning is magnified considerably when the learning process is directly connected to achieving the greater Purpose. People become even more motivated to become self-directed learners when they perceive that they can and should control the means of achieving the compelling Purpose they have previously embraced. As such, self-directed learning isn't a theoretical exercise, but a specific means of accomplishing something important. Aided by the star content in the Path to Mastery and the Principles, the potential self-directed learner can be confident of becoming both a self-directed learner and a great leader.

The neuroscience of learning and mass customization is used to transition these now unfrozen learners to be fully self-directed learners. As we mentioned before, all learning is the wiring of neurons into patterns that occur most efficiently through frequent, short, very practical, and highly personal learning experiences. Becoming a great learner and great leader means practicing attitudes and behaviors consistently, in small increments, and, ideally, in a group setting that drives reflective thinking. As people create their own and their group's leadership program, they are experiencing many repetitions of self-directed learning.

Mass customization of the learning experiences provides many more personalized repetitions in ways that teach self-directed learning while also teaching leadership. When applied to learning, everyone holds the same key ideas, yet the Learning Tasks are unique to each person. The learner understands the Purpose, Mastery, and Principles of great leadership—the "mass" part—and adapts them to create immense personal value—the "customization" part. Thus, the learner is guided through frequent, powerful, highly repetitive individual and group learning experiences that teach self-directed learning.

The bigger picture perspective on all of this science is that self-directed learners and great leaders are thoughtful, frequently reflecting on what they are doing and why they are doing it. In turn, reflection drives the literal wiring of the neurons to create fully internalized leadership behaviors. Teaching people to be self-directed reflective learners is also teaching them to be great long-term self-directed, thoughtful leaders.

AFFIRMATIVE LEADERSHIP AND SELF-DIRECTED LEARNING

Any instructional designer will tell you that it is impossible to create a learning program that works for everyone in all situations. Even the Affirmative Leadership Learning Tasks crafted in Chapter 4 are inherently too generic to be truly practical and valuable to every individual. The premise of the Affirmative Leadership approach, and the implication of all the aforementioned science, is that the learners must direct their own learning. They must understand the intent of their Learning Tasks and adapt them to their own situations to have meaningful learning and leadership development experiences. Through this process, learners are taught self-directed learning as well as many specific Affirmative Leadership attitudes and behaviors.

In Affirmative Leadership, becoming a truly self-directed learner begins when the group adapts the Learning Tasks for Big Step 1 to their own situations. More specifically, the second part of the Affirmative Leadership Launch Workshop reinforces the drive to self-directed learning that inspires the Learning Group to own their learning program. The facilitator instructs the Learning Group to quickly skim through the entire task list for Big Step 1, reflect on the overall purpose of this set of Learning Tasks, and share it with their group. For example, at a safety consulting firm, they read out loud and reviewed the following list:

1. Write one or two sentences about what it means to be a great safety leader. Include a statement about why this is important for me personally and as a safety leader.
2. Write about two company objectives that conflict with my safety responsibilities. Develop a strategy to reconcile the conflicts while maintaining my standard to be a great safety leader.

3. Identify two situations when I have been pressured to compromise safety. Develop a strategy to ensure that I have the courage to overcome the opposition and not compromise my standards.

4. List three qualities of a strong leader. Explain how I can gain by demonstrating these qualities.

5. Interview someone who always demonstrates commitment to safety. Learn three things that will help me to increase my commitment.

6. Describe why it is important to be trusted as a safety leader in my company.

Their coach led them through the ensuing discussion. Joe, one of the participants, commented that these Learning Tasks were all about getting him to understand the reasons the organization should be dedicated to safety. Susan, one of his colleagues, built on Joe's comment by stating, *"It is more than just an understanding. It is being able to talk about it with confidence."* Others contributed. Interpreting the intent of the learning and the resulting discussion causes the learner to step into the shoes of the stars and start to think like self-directed learners.

After five minutes of discussion, the facilitator tells the coaches to lead the Learning Group to review the Principles for each task, understand the intent of the Learning Task, and adapt it to make it personal and valuable. Here Affirmative Leadership gets more demanding. Each learner and the Learning Group as a whole must understand and adapt each Learning Task, keeping the time required for the Learning Task to a maximum of one hour per task, and ideally just thirty minutes.

For example, one group of safety consultants had to interview a long-time lead consultant about some guiding principles and values of the organization. The coach said, *"What is the intent of this Learning Task? Remember the tie to the Principle."*

They responded:

"To understand how some of our top people think about the job."
"To hear in their words what it means to work here."
"To get some of their wisdom."

They discussed the best way to get a broad perspective from several people and decided that each person would organize a ten-minute interview with one company leader, asking her to join a weekly group conference call. The coach tested them: *"Are you convinced this will be a valuable learning experience? If your answer is no, let's change it until all of you can answer yes."*

Everyone thought it was valuable and was directed to write a note about the intent and the adaptation, anchoring the decisions. As they discussed the intent of the stars, adapted the Learning Tasks, and recorded their agreements, the group gained a deeper appreciation for the reasoning behind the activity and its benefits to them.

They repeated this process for each Learning Task in the Big Step. By the end, they had a highly personalized plan for the first month that linked Principles to Learning Tasks and the Learning Tasks to each other. Never once in this process is learning pushed at anyone. An idea is presented; the group is asked what the stars intended; and then the group adapts the task to make it worthwhile for them. This provides the platform to both organize and present the tasks. The "make it work for you" methodology enables learners to first think about the task and then to adapt it.

While most learners require only a short time to understand the process and embrace it enthusiastically, some learners are shocked by the expectations and resist the process. As one learner put it, *"I expect to be told things in a class and then decide if I will use what was presented. I don't expect to have to work this hard or be this responsible for the class."* Someone like this is probably not a good candidate for a leadership role.

When a learner adapts a Learning Task to make it work for him, he becomes more committed to actually performing the task, which is self-directed learning. Furthermore, the social learning, high number of repetitions of the content and learning process, and intense reflection in this process cause deeper understanding and require more participation and ownership. Cumulatively, a lot of learning, including development of self-directed learning, occurs (Figure 6-2).

Once the foundation of meaningful self-directed learning has been established, other leadership skills are developed. First, the group must agree to a weekly meeting time. While this may sound trivial, it is always an obstacle to an effective group learning experience. When members live in different time zones, work different shifts, or can't work outside of defined hours without compensation, finding a time that's convenient for everyone can be challenging. Even without

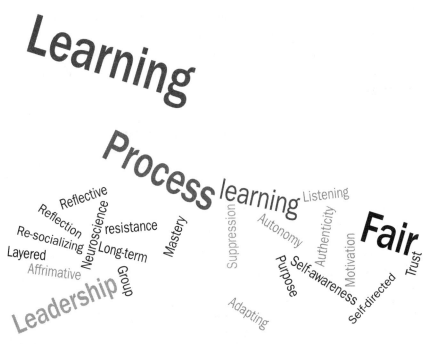

FIGURE 6-2. Development of self-directed learning.

these issues, most people are so heavily scheduled that adding another meeting, no matter how valuable it is, feels like a burden.

Our experience is that weekly meetings are best. More frequent meetings interfere with regular work schedules too much. Less frequent meetings make it too hard to stay focused on the program. Groups just have to work through the scheduling, although it is important that the group understands that the most effective Learning Groups meet weekly for the duration of the program.

This sets the stage for yet another review, this time to assign each Learning Task to specific dates. The coach leads the group to review the modified Learning Tasks and decide when they should be completed. The guideline is one to two tasks per week with a Big Step taking four to five weeks. Some weeks the group may do one Learning Task while other weeks they may do three. They are told that they must do at least one task per week because learning occurs most efficiently with frequent small repetitions, but also not to try to do too much each week as this will overload their learning and discussions. The group sets a target start and completion date for every Learning Task.

During the scheduling discussion, the program's time requirements become real, and people start worrying that it will add to already overcommitted schedules. As one person put it, "*I am already so loaded, I just can't see adding another task to my list.*"

However, when they adapt the learning tasks, they also see that because they're part of what they should be doing anyway, the additional time is actually minimal. For example, a large insurance organization that put 4,000 frontline leaders through an Affirmative Leadership program experienced an actual incremental requirement of about six hours per month, but because the Learning Tasks were so integrated with ongoing work, the time required was not perceived as a burden.

While setting the meeting times and scheduling tasks seem mainly administrative, they also teach learners to be self-directed. Leaders always have to establish priorities and manage schedules, which includes setting priorities for learning and scheduling. In most organizations, learning is given a low priority and scheduling is driven by the instructor's availability for classes or personal availability for computer use. Affirmative Leadership makes learning a priority by setting up and helping people manage several time-related challenges to the learning process. Self-directed learning requires that learning be given a priority and be scheduled, both of which are, of course, critical leadership behaviors. As a senior manager put it, *"Great leaders are also great at managing priorities and schedules."*

Even the administration portions of Affirmative Leadership teach great self-directed learning and leadership.

LEARNING TASKS FOR GETFABULOUS!

At GetFabulous!, once the Learning Groups have gone through the Principles, the groups are beginning to think the way the stars do about being a great store manager. Then Charles asks them to focus on the Learning Tasks. Before they leap in, he shows them how to get the most from their efforts by reviewing a list of Principles and related Learning Tasks. The Learning Tasks were developed by the stars, Charles, and Betty, and they are the practice exercises that the learners will work on for the next several weeks. Each task links to a Principle, refers to supporting documentation where it has been included, and has start and complete dates.

After going over the list, Charles describes the process of reviewing and adapting the tasks in the following sequence:

1. Read through all of the learning tasks for this big step to get a feel for the things you will be doing over the next month and see how they link back to the principles.
2. Go back to the learning tasks starting at the top, read each one, and discuss the intent of each task: the outcome that the stars wanted you to get.
3. Adjust or adapt each task to make sure that you do get the intended result from the task but also keep the learning task to less than an hour—thirty minutes is better. Make it work for you!
4. Establish your weekly meeting times.
5. Create a schedule for the next month or so by setting the start and finish dates that work for you and the group.

By leading the groups to discuss the intent and adapt the tasks to create personal value, Charles and the coaches have transitioned the ownership of the learning process to the store managers. The social aspects of the learning process create a buzz within the group. They are leaning forward, listening closely to each other, and working intensely to develop a great learning program. Their individual excitement for taking control is shared by the group as a supportive learning team. They are learning to be self-directed learners and leaders simultaneously.

Charles moves them on again. He guides them to establish a meeting time for the weekly debriefing and to schedule the events. He gives them the parameters:

Meet once a week for no more than one hour.
Do at least one Learning Task per week—more if it makes sense to group tasks.
Take no more than five weeks to finish the Big Step.

As with virtually every group, setting the weekly meeting time is the biggest problem, with people making comments like *"I can meet Tuesdays at 3:00"* or *"Wednesdays at 8:30, but not Tuesdays at 3:00."*

Typically, they resolve this within ten minutes because so many of them realize that this program is more important than most conflicting activities and events.

USING REFLECTIVE LEARNING TO CREATE THE BIG PICTURE

Reflection brings all the different elements of the Affirmative Leadership process into an integrated whole. It takes time and attention to learn to reflect and to do it regularly.

In Affirmative Leadership, group discussions and recorded learning both encourage reflection. Learners use reflection throughout the process. They discuss and write about their Purpose, Path to Mastery, Principles, and Learning Tasks. These are done as separate topics in order to reduce the amount and complexity of the information that must be included in the reflections and, as a result, make learning the new reflective skills easier. Each time people do this, they learn more about leadership and strengthen their reflective abilities.

All of the work with the stars and the earlier portions of the Launch Workshop build to a crescendo in the third and final segment of the Launch Workshop. The learners are guided to reflect on the totality of their experience, record three to four of their most important learnings, and share them with their Learning Group. This requires them to reflect on all aspects of the six-hour session, evaluate the relative importance of and connections between the different sections, distill the most important ones, and process them into writing and a short presentation. They must be reflective in order to perform this closing exercise; and much of that reflection is about learning and leadership:

- All the underlying science comes into play in this last section. **Fair process** is shown throughout, from the expectation that people can integrate and maintain large complex conceptual structures to the administration of a Learning Task schedule.

- **Motivation 3.0** (Purpose, Mastery, and Autonomy) motivates people to synthesize their learnings and become self-directed learners.
- **Multiple reflections** on positive images, discussions, and written recordings of learning create the repetitions necessary to rewire the neural circuits and create long-term positive habits.
- **Mass customization** allows the concepts to be centrally defined but locally and personally applied.

This last section becomes the capstone for self-directed learning. At GetFabulous!, Charles has the groups open their Learning Journals. He asks for a brief response about what they did in each topic. He talks about Purpose, Path to Mastery, Principles, and Learning Tasks. People make comments such as:

"Purpose was where we talked about connecting with our clients and improving their lives."
"Path to Mastery is where we defined the overall big steps or phases of the process, with some really good ideas."
"Principles is where we talked a lot about our personal experiences and the meaning of being a great store manager."
"In Learning Tasks we defined our learning program."

Charles continues: *"Reflecting on the whole day and the learning process, write three to four things that are your most important takeaways from the day—what you think are the most important learnings from the day. After you have written them down, you will share them with your Learning Group."*

The silence in the room is remarkable after a day of such intense discussions. People are leaning forward, clearly processing information. As the training manager later commented: *"You could really see their mental wheels turning."*

After a few minutes, Charles asks the coaches to lead a time of sharing with their groups. Tremendous ideas emerge:

> *"I never had a learning experience like this. It is much more demanding than any training class but it is really good. I particularly liked the Principles discussion as I got a lot of good ideas from the group. I am going to talk a lot about connecting with clients and making a difference in their lives."*
>
> *"I didn't really have a strong idea of my Purpose as a store manager. I was just trying to make numbers. I can see how having a stronger Purpose and connecting it to the Learning Tasks would really make a difference. I also see that my attitude is really the driver of the store culture. If I treat my team with dignity, they will treat our customers with dignity."*
>
> *"I was a little freaked out by the Learning Tasks and defining my own learning. But I can see how I have to take charge more of my learning and my store. I have to be a learner and a leader."*

In the sharing that follows, learners often credit their coach and their peers with great insight and support. They celebrate everyone's contribution even as they receive kudos for their own work. All it takes to close the workshop is a few kind words from Charles and the coach. After just six hours of work, they are on their way to becoming great self-directed learners and amazing store managers.

The Launch Workshop ends with closing remarks by the facilitator and coaches, complimenting people and tying the discussion back to the greater Purpose. At GetFabulous!, the remarks focused on connecting with customers and creating a great place to work. The groups were smiling, laughing, and obviously feeling great about their experience.

The coaches usually feel great too, but often have many comments and questions about their experience. They put a lot of energy into the coaching and want to know if they did it well. They also need to decompress. The facilitator uses all of the sciences to help the coaches become better self-directed learners and leaders.

So after the workshop, the facilitator asks the coaches how they felt the day went. Typically, coaches begin by expressing surprise at how well it went and how engaged everyone was. Most had expected the approach to be difficult, bordering on disastrous, and they were pleasantly surprised when their Learning Groups responded with energy and insight. While they still aren't sure why it went so well, they feel they have already made a contribution.

The facilitator takes a few minutes to tie their response back to the Purpose, which is becoming a reality.

Sometimes, though fortunately not too often, issues such as the following arise:

"Joe (a participant) *just wouldn't contribute to the group and made lots of negative comments about 'he already knew all of this.' "*
or
"Sarah was clearly uncomfortable adjusting the tasks."

The coaches spend a little time with sharing ideas on how to handle these situations. In most cases, resistance to the Affirmative Leadership process is discomfort about changing from a passive learner to a self-directed learner. Affirmative Leadership is very demanding, and some people just don't want to work that hard. In most cases, these people are given a choice of either changing their attitude or dropping out of the program.

After this discussion, the coaches return to their Leading Group Learning coach training program and record three to four learnings about being a coach. Here are some of the recorded learnings from the coaches at GetFabulous!:

"I had a hard time not jumping in and talking. Once we got started, the ideas were so good that I wanted to participate. But I noticed that when I talked, they didn't, so I shut up."

"This is such a different way of leading. I can see how I should be using this with everyone. I give them structure and room to learn, but I also insist that they learn. This is very different from just focusing on a store's numbers."

"I liked this program a lot. I have never seen my managers so excited. I began to see how I needed to be the role model for their learning and leadership. If I am a great learner and leader, they are more likely to become great learners and store leaders too, and this will pass this on to their teams."

The coaches were still a little uncertain about how this would all play out, but most of them also had the swagger of increased confidence. The Launch Workshop is the beginning of great leadership for coach and learner alike.

CONCLUSION

Humans are at their best when they are deeply motivated to achieve something greater than themselves. When people have this motivation, they work incredibly hard to become great at what they do. Great leaders are motivated this way and inspire others to have similar feelings. Far too much of organizational learning extinguishes these motivations and in doing so creates barriers to leadership development.

The Affirmative Leadership Launch Workshop changes this by using science to guide people to discover something dormant in their selves—their love for learning. As their love of learning flourishes, they easily learn many of the attitudes and behaviors of great leaders. As one participant put it:

"This was totally different than what I expected but I loved it. I have never felt so appreciated as a learner and a poten-

tial leader. I loved being able to drive my own program, and thought what is in the program is great."

The Launch Workshop is only the first step in a process that takes months, but it is a powerful step toward something of great value for any organization: a culture where everyone is a self-directed learner and a great Affirmative Leader.

But there is an even more important impact of a Launch Workshop that comes from being a self-directed learner and leader, expressed by Mayumi, a first-line customer service manager from a Japanese company: *"That was the fastest six hours of training I have ever experienced. It was quick, engaging, and just plain fun. I look forward to what comes next."*

LEARNING TO LEAD

USING PRACTICAL EXERCISES AND LEARNING GROUPS
TO MAKE THE NEW LEARNING STICK

Angela was already a very good program manager and was not excited about her department's Affirmative Leadership program. The program was five months long, and over the course of it Angela had to record what she had learned from the activities to build her skills. The final task was: *"Print out your learning journal and highlight all of the things that positively affected your job performance over the past five months."* She was shocked when she printed out forty-three pages. She had highlighted over two-thirds of the document as being beneficial to her performance. Her performance dramatically improved. and she is now an advocate of Affirmative Leadership.

All learning entails conscious practice. The Affirmative Leadership Launch Workshop is only, as its name suggests, the beginning of an Affirmative Leadership program. What follows, as described in this chapter, will be a number of weeks (the time frame varies) of weekly practical exercises, guided by coaches and built on the insights, attitudes, and frameworks developed in the Workshop.

When people take control of their own learning and consciously practice emulating the stars, their goals, reactions, and behaviors change. The leader that is inside each person emerges.

This chapter shows:

- How the Affirmative Leadership approach uses applied tasks, discussions, reflective learning, and anchoring of that learning to create new and purposeful long-term habits in both the coaches and their Learning Groups
- The methodologies used to bring about sustained learning

The chapter concludes with how science and methodology come together in a real situation at GetFabulous!.

THE SCIENCE OF SUSTAINED LEARNING

All learning is the wiring or rewiring of neurons in the brain. Behaviors and attitudes are formed by frequent, consistent, and conscious practice over time. Eventually, the new neural connections and patterns overtake and displace the old ones, and the learner thinks and behaves in new ways.

Neuroscience has shown that frequent repetition of a key concept, attitude, or behavior causes neurons to fire simultaneously, which wires them together. This consistent firing and rewiring in the brain provide the basis for long-term storage of new ideas. The model applies to all learning—chess, military tactics, management, sports, or any other specific skill. Researchers call the brain's ability to wire and rewire "neuroplasticity."

Many other neural factors affect our ability to learn. We've already discussed how positive images cause the release of dopamine that generates a sense of well-being and an openness to learning, while negative images stimulate the release of cortisol in the "fear" portions of the brain that cause resistance to learning. We've also discussed the power of social learning—how individuals participating in social groups learn differently and more efficiently than in isolation. There is also an optimum amount of new information people can process. Too much information too fast overloads short-term memory and the prefrontal cortex while too little information too slowly allows attention to wander. In addition, the brain processes linked hierarchies of information (that is, big concepts supported by smaller concepts, supported by still smaller concepts) more quickly than in other approaches. New neuroscience findings give substantial guidance in how to optimize the value of a learning experience.

Combining the neuroscience, much of which has been summarized by Rock, with Pink's Motivation 3.0 creates a learning experience that is far more effective than traditional approaches to learning. The new learning methodology suggested by this research and embedded in Affirmative Leadership uses many small repetitions of positive images, particularly of the compelling Purpose, to generate a better neural response. When positive images are created and things are practiced consciously in a group setting, learning becomes much more effective and efficient, and Mastery develops faster than was previously thought possible.

AFFIRMATIVE LEADERSHIP'S GUIDED PRACTICUM

Practice makes perfect. Affirmative Leadership guides systematic individual and group practice of the stars' images until they are fully internalized. It does this by following a consistent weekly process called the Guide Practicum. Learners are guided to "do" a Learning Task, "discuss" what they did and what they learned in a group setting, and "anchor" their learnings in their Learning Journal. Do-Discuss-Anchor efficiently provides many repetitions of the desired attitudes and behaviors. During Do-Discuss-Anchor, learners are given lots of guidance on how to optimize the value of the many repetitions for learning any Affirmative Leadership role.

At the end of the safety consulting firm's Launch Workshop

discussed in Chapter 6, learners customized and scheduled their Learning Tasks for the next four to six weeks. Each of these tasks drives multiple brain repetitions, and each repetition is a discrete event that is gentle on the prefrontal cortex and short-term memory. For example, the first week's tasks for a safety leadership program are:

- Write one or two sentences about what it means to be a great safety leader. Include a statement about why this is important for me personally and as a safety leader.
- Write about two company objectives that conflict with my safety responsibilities. Develop a strategy to reconcile the conflicts while maintaining my standard of being a great safety leader.

Both Learning Tasks were slightly modified by the Learning Groups in the Launch Workshop. One group thought it would be more powerful and compelling to make a video about their commitment to safety leadership rather than just write a statement. Another group wanted one conflict to come from within the company (for example, time to ensure safety versus billable hours) and another to be in the client's environment (for example, commitment to safety versus production deadlines). They also decided to present their analyses, including their strategies for managing the potential conflicts, as a table in PowerPoint so it would be easy for everyone to understand. The customization process guided both groups to multiple repetitions of the key concepts while increasing the value of the assigned Learning Tasks.

Beginning the first week after the Launch Workshop, the Learning Group follows the Do-Discuss-Anchor process. Each week, learners do the tasks and prepare to report their experiences to the group. This is the "do" portion of Do-Discuss-Anchor. The safety leadership learners wrote out or videoed their statements and thought through how to present them. Next, they conducted their analyses and prepared their presentations. Doing these things didn't take much time but required small, realistic applications of the concepts. Preparing to present what they had done provided two more repetitions—analyzing what to say and preparing to say it. Thus, each learning task repeated the star attitudes and behaviors six times in short, easily processed increments.

In the "discuss" portion of Do-Discuss-Anchor, social learning dominates. Each learner presents their experience from doing the Learning Task and describes what they learned. People listen intently to each other and, with the guidance of the coach, compare each presentation to their own experience, highlighting differences and distilling the commonalities. For example, for the first task, Jorge, a safety coordinator, wrote about how losing one of his workers and having to tell the man's young pregnant wife that her husband was dead created a fanatical commitment to never being in that situation again. Marta, a consultant based in Qatar supervising safety on drilling platforms, said that her conflict with the client was religious and social. A small woman (she is 5'2") and not a Muslim, she was frequently challenged by physically bigger men, who thought the platforms were not for women. The group then talked about how a deep commitment to safety would transcend the issues and ultimately lead to her acceptance. The coach asked probing questions to elicit group participation and response and drive for greater depth of reflection.

Most of the work done for Learning Tasks has this gritty realism. People give each other emotional support and suggest strategies. For example, a video made by safety consultant Chu Mei Woo was such a powerful statement about the importance of being a safety leader that others in her Learning Group circulated it until the video went viral within the company and was formally incorporated into the new hire orientation. The "discuss" portion of Do-Discuss-Anchor drives multiple additional repetitions of how to lead effectively in these complex and challenging environments.

Also, when one person does a task and reflects on it, the person has one experience. When a group of people do the task and share their reflections, they each have multiple experiences. This multiplier effect of social learning dramatically affects the learning curve.

Now moving into "anchor," the coaches guide the group's intense engagement and thinking into conscious learning. Coaches ask, *"What did you learn from this experience?"* This is a surprisingly difficult question for people to answer because it is a break from passive learning. Their first response is usually to describe what they did. Chu Mei Woo, for instance, said: *"I made a video."* The coach replies with: *"That is what you did. Now tell me what you learned from doing it."*

There is almost always a long silence when the learners finally understand this question. They're used to classes in which they merely nod their heads and go on to the next thing. Being asked to consciously identify what they've learned, discuss it, and record it is different. But after a pause, most can do it. Here are some examples:

From Mohammed (writing about his learnings from the first task): *I learned that I have to view safety more from a moral perspective than from a compliance perspective. My emotional commitment will be more important to my success than any paperwork, though I have to be good with the paperwork too. Safety has to be my state of being.*

From Jessica: *I have to better own my development. I always feel pressure to keep my billings up, but I am doing that at a loss of balance. I am squeezing out my own development, which hurts me and ultimately hurts the company.*

These are typical insights in that they stress the judgments and tradeoffs everyone makes—the real issues and skills of leadership.

Writing about what is learned drives still deeper reflection, reinforces positive images, facilitates passage through short-term memory, and gives more repetitions. If people have created materials such as the videos, and are using persuasive technology, they can usually attach these materials to their learnings to create a complete record of their experience. Good journal entries are concise and focus on what people learned from the activity and how they benefited from it.

Do-Discuss-Anchor uses the neuroscience of learning in many subtle ways to boost learning of the desired attitudes and behaviors.

WORKING ON EACH BIG STEP

The group repeats the Do-Discuss-Anchor for each set of tasks in each Big Step. They review the driving Principles, understand the learning intent of the task, adapt the task to create extraordinary learning value, revise the schedule, do the task, discuss it, and record what they have learned. Each task builds on the previous task within a Big Step, reinforcing the earlier learning while becoming progressively more demanding and sophisticated as the sequence builds more leadership attitudes and skills. For example, Marta leveraged her work on Learning Task 1 to deal with discrimination in Learning Task 2. A hierarchy of attitudes and skills is gradually building. Here is an example of how the repetitions build from a program for restaurant managers:

RESTAURANT OF CHOICE: My commitment to providing every guest with an awesome dining experience and every team member with a great work experience is the foundation for guest loyalty and financial success. We provide a great experience that improves our guests' quality of life and are a well-run, profitable business.

MOTIVATED TEAM: I develop and lead a highly motivated team that is dedicated to providing great food and amazing service. We work together to ensure that every customer experience is awesome.

EFFICIENT SYSTEMS: I ensure that all my operational systems perform at optimum levels. I understand and communicate to the team the importance of using the systems as designed in order to ensure guest satisfaction and restaurant profitability.

AWESOME GUEST EXPERIENCE: I am a role model for emotionally connecting with each guest. Guests know I care and that every team member cares, and this creates a great dining experience. We provide excellent food and service and are fast and effective at service recovery (if needed).

OPTIMIZE PROFITABILITY: I own the financial success of the business. I understand and manage the tension between cost management and the guest experience, balancing the costs of the business with ensuring a great guest experience. I effectively manage food and labor costs, ensuring that our costs are always well controlled without jeopardizing the guest experience.

BIG SALES GROWTH: I leverage national promotional efforts and develop local promotional campaigns that further sustain guest loyalty and attract many new guests. I make the restaurant the first choice for families, sports teams, clubs, and other events. People want to come to my restaurant and select us over all of the competition.

Each incremental Learning Task and Big Step expands and reinforces the earlier learning, driving deeper internalization.

The coaches play an important role in managing this developmental sequence. At the end of each big step, the coaches review their group's recorded learning and determine if the learner is ready to advance to the next step. In many organizations, they are required to formally confirm that a learner has demonstrated enough understanding of the current Big Step to advance to the next one. Being held accountable in this way is often shockingly new for the coaches, and for those told they're not ready for the next Big Step.

For instance, Karen, a coach at a large pharmaceutical company, decided that Walter was simply not trying hard enough. She told him that she would not be advancing him with the rest of the group until he showed her he had a better attitude and was using the star content in his job. Confronting Walter's undesirable attitude and behavior was hard for Karen, but her reputation was on the line and she wasn't going to risk it by giving Walter an undeserved pass. So she was very clear that Walter was not getting confirmed on Big Step 1 until he had clearly learned the content of the program and was using it consistently.

For Walter, this was stunning feedback. He had a long history of cruising through training and his job. This was one of the few times in his professional life that he had been held accountable for learning and performance. Nervously, Karen talked to him about missed opportunities and the consequences of not trying; Walter responded. He became much more involved, and eventually became a leader of the Learning Group. Karen learned as much from this experience as Walter did, which is quite common.

The coaches' influence increases when the organization tracks the learners' progress and learning by having executives attend some of the weekly meetings and requesting progress reports. If the organization uses persuasive technology, executives usually have a "dashboard" summarizing progress and learning. This monitoring makes it easier to support the coaches, increases the coaches' accountability, and tells all participants that the organization is committed to the program.

KEEPING THE MOMENTUM GOING

Neural conflict between established old habits and developing new ones becomes an outright barrier to progress after about six to eight weeks of the program. New habits are not yet established and old ones are still there. You know you are in this conflict when learners say things like: *"This is too hard,"* *"This is taking too much time,"* and *"I just don't see the value in this."* These comments, and the feeling of discomfort they express, are signs that the brain is defending the old habits—a biological response. We tell people: *"This is the old habits fighting the new habits. Keep going and it will go away soon."* These comments and the discomfort disappear with some conscious interventions and support and after about two more weeks of practice and Learning Tasks.

One of the most important aspects of any change initiative is keeping the momentum going when people hit this barrier and start to lose their focus in the program. The Midpoint Checkpoint meeting that occurs around the completion of Big Step 2 is designed to address the neural barrier. The Midpoint Checkpoints are with only one Learning Group at a time as the groups have already formed and are more open about their comments with familiar people. Mixing Learning Groups tends to suppress participation.

The Midpoint Checkpoint has three objectives:

1. Boost commitment by the learners and the coaches to the program
2. Quickly identify and adjust to any issues that emerge from the session
3. Introduce the next level of self-directed learning, which we call "meta-learnings"

The first part of the Midpoint Checkpoint is a discussion of the Learning Group's progress to date. People share elements of the program that are creating benefit and adjust areas that aren't. This is another instance of Fair Process. By asking for genuine feedback on the program, and making adjustments in response to that feedback, the organization communicates its respect for the learners' perspectives.

The most common positive comments are that the group discussions are helpful and that the tasks are practical. The problems that arise are usually about having to adjust the Learning Tasks and that the Learning Tasks demand time. When people say things like *"We really had to change the task to accommodate (time, schedule, situation),"* they sound guilty. Their tone of voice shows that they feel they are doing something wrong. When we remind them that they are *supposed to* adjust the tasks and to manage their own time, they are surprised but pleased.

These comments are so consistent that they are actually a setup for the next part of the Checkpoint, which advances the learners' ability to self-direct. In this second part, learners are shown what they are actually learning, the "meta-learnings." Meta-learnings can't be taught at the beginning of the program; they must be experienced to be fully understood. The three meta-learnings that are presented in the Midpoint Checkpoint are:

Meta Learning #1: You Own Your Learning
Meta Learning #2: Reflection Creates Power
Meta Learning #3: Great Leadership Is Mastering the Intangibles

The main points discussed are that self-directed learners make better leaders and that taking responsibility for their learning program is part of learning to be a leader. As people become self-directed, they become more reflective, which builds the critical leadership attributes of authenticity and trust. The Midpoint Checkpoint closes with a discussion about how the first two meta-learnings are about the intangibles of leadership, how they make the difference between great and mediocre leadership, and finally, why the remaining Big Steps will be much more challenging because they focus on these intangibles.

The typical response to the meta-learning discussion is first a stunned silence followed by an excited buzz. As one person put it; *"I thought something more was going on but couldn't quite see it. This is great how the program is teaching us how to be leaders by guiding us to actually think and act like leaders."* This results in a big boost in engagement and participation. This is particularly true for the more experienced people, who often make comments such as: *"Now this is an interesting idea."*

More importantly, the Midpoint Checkpoint drives a measurable increase in impact. In organizations that are using ongoing measures of performance and correlating these measures to progress through the Big Steps, there is an obvious and important change to the learning curve. While there is consistent steady progress up to the Midpoint Checkpoint, after the checkpoint results soar upwards. This result has been found in all Affirmative Leadership programs, from demand forecast accuracy in a customer service group to sales in a retail organization to launching spacecraft to the outer planets.

GUIDED PRACTICUM AT GETFABULOUS!

The guided Practicum at GetFabulous! illustrates the power of the process. Each week after their successful Launch Workshop, the GetFabulous! groups meet and discuss what they learned from their tasks. Jenni, the coach of one of the teams of store managers (SMs), leads the weekly conference call and the SMs join the meeting from their own stores. Jenni follows the Do-Discuss-Anchor process.

"*Can someone please read the first Learning Task we were work-ing on this past week?*" asks Jenni.

Tom, an SM, replies, "*Write a vision statement for the store. (See example.) Discuss the vision with the DM and then share with the sales team.*"

"*Did we adapt this task in any way?*"

"I did," said Susan, another SM. "*I had my assistant store manager help me create our vision statement and we both presented it to our regional manager.*"

"*Great! Why don't you start by sharing your vision statement, and the rest of you listen for things you liked about the statement.*"

Jenni is getting the discussion going by prompting the other SMs to listen carefully and consider ideas other than their own.

Susan shares her vision statement: "*We believe that our guests deserve the best care and ideas that we can offer so they can present themselves to others in a way that makes us all proud. We respect each other and work each day to the best of our abilities.*"

She receives applause from the other SMs, and then the group immediately starts to comment on the ideas that she presented: using the word "guests," giving the guests "best care," showing them "respect," and helping them "present themselves." Jenni adds, "*Nice job! If she has an idea that you like and you want to add it to your statement, please do.*"

They continue to share their statements, borrowing ideas from one another. Jenni asks people to comment on key ideas and encourages the learners to listen to and respond to each other. At the end, Jenni asks, "*What did you all learn from this task?*" This moves the discussion from "here is what I did" to "this is what I learned from doing." The group takes a few seconds, and then people begin to talk:

> "*I learned that having a vision helps me to set a standard of per-formance in the store.*"
> "*I learned that my vision was different from the vision my regional*"

manager had, and we had a great discussion about where we were heading."
"I learned that my sales team really wanted to have that target and vision. It helps them understand why I ask so much of them."

At the end, Jenni asks everyone to anchor their insights in their Learning Journal by describing at least one thing they discovered from the discussion. Then they discuss and anchor their learnings about the week's second Learning Task.

Jenni asks them to read the tasks scheduled for the following week to see if they need to adapt them. She is preparing them for the next Do-Discuss-Anchor cycle by reviewing and adapting the next week's Learning Tasks. Do-Discuss-Anchor becomes a rhythm that the group gets used to very quickly. Later, Jenni discovers that her team can continue Do-Discuss-Anchor even in her absence.

At week five in the program, Jenni and her team are ready to complete the first Big Step and move on to the second. The SMs have spent time cementing their personal vision stories and are now ready to look at the best practices for growing the skills and talents of their sales associates.

Before anyone moves to Big Step 2, Jenni reviews the quality and depth of her group's Big Step learnings. Jenni is formally accountable for ensuring that each SM in her learning group has internalized and applied the ideas from Big Step 1. She is pleased with their progress and formally confirms that each member of the group is ready to advance to Big Step 2. Her accountability for the effectiveness of the group's learning experience makes her a better, more conscientious coach.

At the next group meeting they open by reading the second Big Step:

GROWING PEOPLE—My success is directly linked to my associates' abilities to connect with our customers. I take every opportunity to teach my team how to create value for our customers.

Jenni's group is excited about this topic. *"I remember talking about this Big Step,"* one store manager said. *"I needed help in developing several of my new associates!"*

The same process is repeated in the second Big Step. The group discusses the meaning of each principle, anchoring what it means to them and discussing why it's important. Each coach and learning group uses this approach, so content and approach are consistent, regardless of the experience or personality of the coaches.

After they have discussed the Principles, the groups review each task's intent and adapt it until they believe the learning experiences will be valuable. They agree on target completion dates. The Do-Discuss-Anchor process continues each week with the group working on a couple of tasks, discussing what they learned, and anchoring their learnings in their learning journals.

As the learning groups get close to the end of Big Step 2, Jenni and the other coaches see that their team members are starting to miss weekly meetings and that some SMs seem listless during meetings—but the coaches respond. They understand the science behind the brain's response when new ways of thinking and behaving are trying to overcome the old. The coaches schedule the Midpoint Checkpoint meetings with their facilitator Charles to help their groups get over the eight-week neural barrier.

Jenni asks Charles to lead part of the Midpoint Checkpoint with her coaches. Charles follows the process of soliciting positive comments as well as concerns about the learning experiences and gets the usual responses about time pressures and discomfort with adapting tasks. He assures everyone that this is normal and that they should just keep working on it and everything will get easier.

He then moves into presenting the three meta-learnings: you own your learning, reflection is power, and master the intangibles. The Learning Group is surprised that in addition to the things they had been working on in the program, they were learning even more important skills. They didn't realize so much was going on behind the scenes. They all write the three meta-learnings and resolve to reflect on them later. Jenni reports that each store manager is more tuned in and energetic about the weekly tasks.

THE STICKINESS OF AFFIRMATIVE LEADERSHIP

For several years, Affirmative Leadership programs ended with a closure presentation. Beginning about two years ago, we started to get requests for extending the program. Learning Groups liked the structure of Do-Discuss-Anchor and wanted to continue to meet. Learning organizations wanted a capability to provide ongoing reinforcement and thought that the infrastructure of coaches and established Learning Groups could be used to rapidly and effectively communicate new information. This was particularly true for organizations facing considerable uncertainty and change. They believed that the Affirmative Leadership infrastructure tightened the coupling between strategic initiatives and action.

This led to the development of an Affirmative Leadership Sustainer program, which extends the best of the star wisdom and Learning Tasks for long-term use. Affirmative Leadership Sustainer begins with a truncated Discovery in which a few of the stars, the project manager, and a few of the coaches review the Principles and Learning Tasks and modify them to provide additional practical reinforcement of the stars' ideas. For example, one of the Sustainer Learning Tasks for GetFabulous! was how to get the most out of seasonal displays. It was a very timely and practical topic that the group could use as a focus for sharing and support.

Having coaches and/or persuasive technology in place also gives the organization the capability to continue to monitor ongoing progress and learning. Once it has the infrastructure, the organization can measure success and see the organization's culture change over an extended time period. As more people grow as Affirmative Leaders, Purpose and Mastery become a deep, engrained part of the culture. The culture of greatness grows and sustains itself.

DISTRIBUTE GLOBALLY, ACT LOCALLY

CREATING LARGE-SCALE, GLOBAL PROGRAMS THAT FEEL LIKE LOCAL CHANGE INITIATIVES

As Simon, the vice president of sales for a global accounting firm, said, *"We have 17,000 account managers in more than 90 countries. We have never found a learning program that could handle our numbers and still have a meaningful impact."*

Teaching six to twenty people is very straightforward—present the knowledge, then follow up with each student to make sure everyone is applying it. But this approach doesn't work with thousands of people who are all over the world. Developing great leadership programs for large numbers of geographically dispersed people requires a sophisticated, but still cost-effective, scaling infrastructure that takes cultural differences into account.

In this chapter, we will:

- Examine some of the challenges scaling presents
- Discuss the underlying science used by Affirmative Leadership to address scaling
- Present Affirmative Leadership solutions for the scaling problem

We will begin with how to develop a basic infrastructure for scaling, add in the complexities of global languages and cultures, and show how, once built, this infrastructure gives organizations the ability to scale new initiatives with great impact and speed at minimal additional cost.

CHALLENGES OF SCALING

Scaling has two elements: easy, inexpensive delivery to large numbers of people and significant impact. Most organizations are so intimidated by the costs of large-scale programs that they focus attention primarily on the cost aspects of a program and less on achieving the desired impact. Of course, they want both, but that balance is rarely evident in discussions of scaling. Reframing the discussion by focusing on effectiveness first, then asking *"how can you do it for large numbers,"* changes the way an organization can approach the scaling problem. Affirmative Leadership uses inexpensive, reliable Web video meeting applications, persuasive technologies, and mass customization to deliver high-impact programs to thousands of people anywhere in the world.

Web meetings reduce the cost but not the impact of instructor-led programs. For example, while sitting in Portland, Oregon, Deborah, a trainer at MegaChip, led Group Learning coach training sessions and Launch Workshops in Asia and Europe. On Sunday, Monday, and Tuesday, she led two-hour Leading Group Learning training for ten Asian and ten European coaches; and on Wednesday and Thursday, she led four Asian and four European six-hour Launch Workshops, each of which had two Learning Groups of eight people. In a week, without any travel expense, she ramped up twenty coaches and kicked off Affirmative Leadership programs for more than 120 candidates on the other side of the world. These Web-delivered Leading Group Learning and Launch Workshops were just as effective as in-person programs.

Persuasive technology makes using Web meetings considerably easier and more effective. Persuasive technologies are Web applications designed to change what people believe and do. Good persuasive technology guides development and completion of a personalized learning program while providing insight for executives into learners' progress. A good persuasive technology that promotes learning typically:

1. Creates and keeps focus on the important learning elements by organizing the expert content in a way that is consistent with the way people learn the best
2. Has learners adapt the star content to fit their particular situation
3. Sets the schedule for completing tasks
4. Records what has been learned from doing the Learning Tasks

The elements that promote scaling are the abilities to:

5. Distribute to many people at once
6. Update centrally and have those updates reach everyone using the technology

One element that is essential for both learning and scaling is the ability of coaches, management, and the learning organization to do the following:

7. Monitor the progress of each Learning Group and individual

Several alternatives for this functionality exist today in software applications, and they have some of the aforementioned abilities. These can be found by searching the general market or through Cerebyte (www.cerebyte.com), which offers a version of a persuasive technology.

By using persuasive technology as part of the Web meeting, learners absorb the content more quickly and internalize it more completely with less effort and expertise from the facilitator. The combination of Web and persuasive technology increases the effectiveness of the learning while decreasing the cost.

Mass customization provides a system for delivering large-scale programs that empower local participation. Most persuasive technologies are designed using elements of mass customization.

Even with mass customization and persuasive technology, there is a trade-off decision between impact and cost. Using facilitators, Web meetings, and persuasive technology for a complete Affirmative Leadership program has greater impact than just using any of these in isolation, but it still entails labor costs. By building an infrastructure of trained coaches using these technologies, long-term costs can be significantly reduced and the speed of deployment can be increased without reducing impact.

BASIC SCALING INFRASTRUCTURE

In Affirmative Leadership, two costs are barriers to scaling: training coaches for group learning and training facilitators for Launch Workshops. Both require an initial investment to build an organization's infrastructure and capability, but the cost decreases significantly in later programs, enabling organizations to get close to the dual goal of high impact and low cost.

When companies use direct managers as the coaches, the process tends to be the most cost effective. In Affirmative Leadership, these managers are taught to become coaches with skills that include cofacilitating the Launch Workshops and monitoring progress. Training managers to be coaches can be expensive, especially if travel is required and professional trainers are hired, but it is very effective.

However, an entire Affirmative Leadership program can be done over the Web, reducing these travel costs. The coaches and learners still get personal interaction with other learners, especially if there are video feeds, and all of the participants can see the faces of the other team members. We have led learning groups comprised of people from different parts of the world, and the only factor that we have found to be difficult is the scheduling of different time zones. Web meetings with videos are an easy, inexpensive way to scale a program.

In addition, most organizations already have a training infrastructure with regional trainers that can be used to train the managers. By training its own trainers, an organization builds a reusable capability for additional programs and increases the effectiveness of these trainers for other training programs. However, building this capability means that traditional trainers must learn to be Affirmative Leaders, which can be challenging for trainers steeped in decades of instructor-led programs.

The Affirmative Leadership "train-the-trainer" program reframes the facilitator experience. New facilitators go through several distinct steps in this order:

- Develop a deep understanding of the underlying science by reading *DRiVE* by Dan Pink, *Your Brain at Work* by David Rock, and *The Power of Positive Deviance* by Richard Pascale, Jerry Sternin, and Monique Sternin
- Learn to be an Affirmative Leader coach by fully participating in a Leading Group Learning coach training class, a Launch Workshop, and an ongoing Guided Practicum, usually by supporting a coach or even as a student coach
- Lead a Launch Workshop (ideally using a persuasive technology) with support from an experienced professional
- Lead a Leading Group Learning coach training class

(again, ideally using a persuasive technology) with support from an experienced professional

The persuasive technology plays an important role in ensuring the impact and lowering the cost of training the trainers and ultimately in developing great Affirmative Leaders. All the trainers need to do is to understand the underlying approach to being an Affirmative Leader and follow the guidance from the technology. They quickly learn to be great Affirmative Leader trainers and become models for their students.

Combining Web meetings, a train-the-trainer approach, a persuasive technology, and phased rollouts creates still more leverage because trainers trained in one region or business unit can be equally effective at leading Affirmative Leadership programs in other regions or units, even if they are physically in different locations. For instance, QuickBurger deployed the restaurant manager Affirmative Leadership program two regions at a time. Regional training and development managers from two regions were trained as part of the rollout for the first two regions, and then these two trainers supported the other regions. More than 180 district managers were taught to lead more than 1,400 restaurant managers in 140 learning groups in a little over two months. Similarly, at MegaChip, a global sales program was implemented in the Americas first, then, in order, in Europe, Japan, the Pacific Rim, and finally China. Most of this was done remotely using Web meetings and only two trainers. Sixty coaches were trained to lead 500 account managers in 60 Learning Groups in about five weeks. In both organizations, large numbers were ramped up very quickly with minimal expense.

Many programs use Web meetings, train-the-trainers, persuasive technology, and phased rollouts. What makes Affirmative Leadership programs different is how reusable the pieces are. Each can be reactivated at very little cost simply by developing a new set of Affirmative Leadership best practices and plugging them into the coaching system. Once the Affirmative Leadership infrastructure is established, any program can be deployed globally to thousands of people in as little as ten days, and with high impact.

ADVANCED SCALING INFRASTRUCTURE: MULTIPLE LANGUAGES, COUNTRIES, AND CULTURES

"We're different!" "You don't know how we do things here." "More #%& from headquarters!"* These are the commonly used expressions of the familiar "not invented here" syndrome. It is human nature to believe that we are special; that our location, our people, and our situation are somehow different from others around the globe. As a result, people and groups tend to believe that centralized programs don't understand their unique situations and will therefore be ineffective if not harmful. Programs that are perceived as locally produced tend to be far more popular than top-down initiatives.

However, local initiatives quickly become ad hoc, and consistency is difficult to maintain across long distances without losing the value of global synergies and standards. Furthermore, in the vast majority of companies, the best practices of the top-performing people in one place work best everywhere else. Organizations need balance between the central and the local, and Affirmative Leadership achieves this through mass customization.

In Affirmative Leadership, local teams make small changes to the stars' articulation of the best practices to better align them with local language, customs, and conditions. This gives local learners more trust in the program; they stop resisting and focus on content. Personalizing and localizing learning thus accelerate the learning process and increase long-term retention.

Inviting stars from around the world to the Wisdom Discovery Workshop is the first step in this global acceptance. Because regional management must use the respect and trust criteria to nominate their stars, the results of the Discovery are more likely to be seen as consistent with the values and needs of the region. This initial willingness to accept the results is further reinforced if regional managers attend the group presentation at the end of the Discovery Workshop and give the stars opportunities to promote the Affirmative Leadership program.

However, bringing in a global team can be expensive and logistically difficult, so relatively few organizations do it. In addition, no matter how extensive the regional participation in a global Discovery is, regions rarely feel that it completely fits their unique situation.

"Delta" Discovery Workshops are a simple, effective way to make the program look and feel completely local. In a Delta Discovery, a few local stars review and mark up the global star wisdom. The local team identifies whatever needs to be changed to optimize the value of the star wisdom for their country, office, language, and so on. While significant changes are rare, the Delta Discovery enables people in different cultures or with different languages to adapt the content in ways that enrich local adoption of the star performers' wisdom and knowledge. The wisdom is perceived as locally developed.

For instance, at a global consulting company, corporate developed a new Affirmative Leadership program that was expected to teach 7,600 people in more than 50 countries how to become great account managers. As with most of their corporate programs, it was developed using only star performers from the United States.

In the past, as Helen the vice president of the Australian region put it, most regions *sat back, listened to whatever was shoved at them, and ignored it because it didn't fit their markets.* So Helen and the other regional vice presidents were shocked when the corporate learning and development team asked each region to participate in a Delta Discovery. Each region was given a best practices document and asked to change anything that wouldn't work in their region. The program became so completely adapted to the language and values of each region that everyone thought it had been developed solely for them. As one of Helen's team said, *"It is nice to see that corporate is finally developing training here in Australia, for Australians!"* All of the other regions felt that the program was theirs, too.

Effectively adapting the learning content to the culture can include adding local colloquialisms, stories, articles, customs, and even references to celebrities. The more the content reflects the essence of the local culture, the better the content will be received. In one instance, while working in Japan, we found that a review group had a lively discussion about the word "authentic." In English, authentic has synonyms such as bona fide, certifiable, certified, dinkum (Australian and New Zealand), genuine, honest, real, right, sure-enough, true, and for real. In Japan, authentic has many more variations, each of which has a different nuance and few of which have an English equivalent. The discussion identified the language and concepts that Japanese learners would understand and embrace most readily.

The example of the differences between English and Japanese raises the issue of local language versus a corporate standard, which can be very challenging. For instance, one global healthcare company developed their best practices in English, but decided to translate both the best practices and the persuasive technology into eight languages, including Korean and Turkish. They decided to do this because the country teams spoke relatively little English and were always complaining that corporate programs were insensitive to their needs. While the commitment to a Delta Workshop for each country eased some of these concerns, translating it all helped the country teams feel valued.

These decisions about language are important to the infrastructure of scaling. Once a decision is made, the organization can accommodate new programs much more quickly and effectively. At QuickBurger, for instance, after an extensive debate about using English, Spanish, or both, the team settled on English and rapidly developed and deployed a sequence of three Affirmative Leadership programs for the restaurant managers: building a great team, ensuring excellent guest service, and optimizing financial performance. Three weeks after completion of the Wisdom Discovery, the programs were guiding 1,400 restaurant managers with minimal additional expense.

Similarly, the first program at the healthcare company required investment to build the infrastructure, but a second program on customer centricity was deployed globally in just a few weeks. The infrastructure provides for scaling and speed.

Yet another language issue surfaces during the Launch Workshops and Guided Practicum. Even if the best practices and persuasive technology are in one language, in our case usually English, most of the Launch Workshop can be done in a local language. For instance, a program for MegaChip, which uses English as its corporate language, kept the customer service best practices, persuasive technology, and facilitation in English but conducted all other discussions in local languages. To make this even more complicated, in China the local language was Cantonese for some and Mandarin for others. A decision was made to use Mandarin, which was the language used by most of the individual contributors. Since many of the learners could read and write English easily but found speaking it difficult, this minimized the language stress and promoted better interactions and learning. However, a bilingual trainer or manager had to help the facilitator understand the dynamics of the group learning. Here, too, once the program was established, follow-on programs occurred rapidly and with minimal English facilitation.

CULTURE AND AFFIRMATIVE LEADERSHIP

Subtle cultural issues also surface during Affirmative Leadership programs that can have a significant impact on scaling. Sometimes these cultural issues promote the Affirmative Leadership structure while at other times they create significant barriers. Because it is inappropriate to overgeneralize any cultural experiences, we will discuss these in the context of specific experiences we have had in implementing Affirmative Leadership in different countries and cultures.

Working on programs in Japan provided some surprising examples of cultural alignment. Having worked in Japan in the 1980s and 1990s, we were aware of the cultural hierarchy of managers and workers and were concerned about how coaching would work. In our previous experience, Japanese managers spoke, and Japanese workers listened. We spent some time with our clients discussing the issue of coaches as facilitators and self-directed learners.

Much to our surprise, creating honor and dignity (that is, Fair Process) resonated very well with the Japanese style of doing business and made the Launch Workshops and Guided Practicum very successful. As a result, the Japanese companies with whom we worked became voracious consumers of Affirmative Leadership, and they proliferated programs to thousands of people around the globe.

Similarly, the discussion aspects of Affirmative Leadership aligned very well with cultures such as those of Spain, Italy, and Israel that stressed verbal skills. The opportunity to verbally explore ideas feels very natural to Learning Groups in these cultures. While all cultures have language, some are more used to using free-flowing language more intensively than others. Often the challenge in these verbal cultures is to ensure that people complete the Learning Tasks and that learnings get recorded as well as discussed.

Another example of this issue can occur in cross-national

Learning Groups in which some of the participants come from cultures in which being verbally aggressive is expected, while others come from cultures in which being verbally aggressive is rude. For example, in a Learning Group with members from several countries, the Chinese and American participants tended to dominate the discussions while the Malaysians and Filipinos were much more reserved. The coach created a safe environment for the Malaysian and Filipino participants by informing them that they would soon be called upon to speak, directly calling on them for comments, and involving them by asking for their reactions to other people's comments. In subtle ways the coach reduced the control by the verbal dominators and increased the participation of the quieter people. There are many good reasons to have truly international Learning Groups but leading them requires some adjustment.

Similarly, mixed gender groups can have very uneven participation, particularly if there are cultural mixes as well. For instance, a group from the safety consulting company had a mix of Middle Eastern and European men and women. The men tended to dominate the conversation and were often condescending to the women, even though the women were just as experienced and skilled. The coach had to work hard to manage the group dynamics, calling on everyone to participate and particularly calling on the men to respond to the women's comments. Initially, this caused some tension, but the coach had explicit support from his management to ensure that his Learning Group practiced gender equality. Over time, everyone realized that each learner had a lot to contribute and the gender imbalances were moderated, though they never fully disappeared. The Affirmative Leadership Learning Group became a vehicle for ensuring that all learners had an equal opportunity to grow into becoming great leaders.

The bigger challenge in many cultures is the coaches, who are used to telling more than listening. Being a great coach is for them, first and foremost, a change to their perception of the manager-employee relationship and to their belief about how people learn. Initially, they don't understand that it is better for them to be coaches than traditional managers. However, as a result of their Leading Group Learning coach training programs and with lots of additional support, coaches realize that their people do better when coached and that they don't have to manage so intensely.

As the coaches become Affirmative Leaders, they realize the benefits of their new attitudes and behaviors. Once they understand the value of coaching, they see that future programs can be implemented quickly and inexpensively. Affirmative Leadership changes work cultures in ways that significantly increase productivity.

When an organization builds its Affirmative Leadership infrastructure, it creates an environment in which impact soars and multiple programs can be delivered fast and inexpensively. The first initiative requires more investment to build, but once built, any Affirmative Leadership program can be scaled to large culturally diverse organizations quickly and effectively.

STEP-BY-STEP BUILDING SCALABLE INFRASTRUCTURE

We love it when executives challenge us about the ability to scale to large diverse groups. We particularly love it when groups of people start off with the "we're different here" conversation. We always agree with them, *You are different, at least that's what we heard from Corporate!"*

We love these challenges because we've seen the following steps work over and over. We have done this process in many organizations with literally hundreds of locations and thousands of people, and we have yet to find a situation where these steps didn't create an infrastructure for high-speed, high-impact scaling of program initiatives.

Step	Process	Outcome
#1: Wisdom Discovery	Conduct a Wisdom Discovery, ideally with star representatives from all critical business units and/or regions.	*Global best practices are defined.*
#2: Delta Wisdom Discovery	Conduct a Delta Discovery for each business unit or region that requires a custom program.	*Localized best practices are defined.*
#3: Coach Selection	Agree to use direct managers as coaches for any role being coached.	*Coaching infrastructure is defined.*
#4: Technology Selection	Select a Web meeting service (if you don't already have one) and a persuasive technology; develop a plan for using both as part of the rollout of your Affirmative Leadership program.	*Technology infrastructure is defined.*
#5: Phased Deployment	Decide the optimum sequence of business units and/or regions for deploying the program; don't try to do too much at once.	*Rollout sequence is defined.*
#6: Train-the-Trainer	Select and prepare a plan for leveraging your current training infrastructure; identify trainers to be trained, particularly ones supporting specific business units or regions; develop and implement your Affirmative Leadership train-the-trainer program.	*Trainers are ready to facilitate Affirmative Leadership programs.*

(continued on page 144)

TABLE 8–1. Twelve-step process for creating the Affirmative Leadership infrastructure.

Step	Process	Outcome
#7: Local Language	Translate the best practices and persuasive technology into local language(s); alternatively, be ready to roll out the best practices in the organization's primary language with the Learning Groups using the local language.	*Local language support is ready.*
#8: Cultural Adaptation	Review the Launch Workshop and Guided Practicum learning processes with the local management team and make any needed adjustments to ensure alignment with the culture.	*Adaptations to cultural norms are understood.*
#9: Leading Group Learning (Coach Training)	Conduct the Leading Group Learning coach training using the trainers or over the Web for all managers who will be coaching.	*Coaches are trained as Affirmative Leader coaches.*
#10: Launch Workshop	Conduct the Launch Workshops using the trainers and/or over the Web to ensure that all potential learners have a compelling Purpose and path to Mastery and have adapted the first Big Step's Principles and Learning Tasks to their environment.	*Leadership candidates have defined their Purpose, path to Mastery, definition of Mastery, and first month's Learning Tasks.*
#11: Guided Practicum	Coaches lead the weekly Learning Tasks; Learning Groups practice reflective learning until the desired attitudes and skills are completely learned; trainers support the coaches during the process.	*Star best practices are learned and applied to the local environment; coaches further develop their leadership.*

Step	Process	Outcome
#12: Certify, Finish, and Sustain	Conduct the closure workshop and complete the certification; celebrate your success; if appropriate, continue on to sustainer.	*Ninety percent of the participants demonstrate the attitudes and behaviors of great Affirmative Leaders.*

TABLE 8-1. Twelve-step process for creating the Affirmative Leadership infrastructure.

Table 8-1 shows a step-by-step guide for creating an infrastructure for the largest, most linguistically and culturally complex organizations. Any of these steps can be modified to fit your unique situation (You, too, can practice mass customization!).

In twelve steps any organization can build an infrastructure for quickly and effectively deploying large-scale, geographically dispersed Affirmative Leadership programs. Using this approach, anyone, anywhere, can experience the impact of a complete Affirmative Leadership program.

These twelve steps have some significant costs. The primary costs are for training the coaches in the Leading Group Learning training class, the time of the participants who are coached, and the facilitator costs of the Launch Workshops. However, the twelve steps also produce the greatest impact for the organization. In an attempt to reduce costs, some organizations will try to shortcut the approach by cutting out some of the twelve steps. While it is likely that they will see better impact than just traditional training alone, or electronic learning alone, it will fall short of the impact of the entire program. Making an initial investment in developing a coaching infrastructure and using the twelve-step approach will pay off with fast and effective future change initiatives.

EXTRAORDINARY SCALING

Once the organization has built the Affirmative Leadership infrastructure, particularly once the coaches are fully motivated and trained to lead their Learning Groups, the costs of scaling decrease sharply without any decrease in its impact. Many of the previous steps can be reduced in scope and cost or skipped entirely, creating extraordinary speed and effectiveness. Here's an example:

Day 1: Heather, the director of transformations for Mega-Chip, gets approval for a program to completely change the business processes and culture of a 1,200-person customer service group spread around five global regions (Americas, Japan, Europe, Pacific Rim, and China). She has less than six months to complete the change.

Days 8–11: A Wisdom Discovery Workshop is conducted in the United Kingdom with twelve stars from the global regions that develop an Affirmative Leadership program for "How to Be a Great Customer Service Representative (CSR)."

Day 16–17: After polishing the new CSR best practices, Jocelyn, the project manager, uses Web meetings to lead three-hour Delta Discovery Workshops for each region. In the Delta Discoveries the best practices are adapted to the language, concepts, markets, and culture of each region.

Day 18–19: Coaches already trained in Affirmative Leadership attend a one-hour coaching refresher webinar. New coaches are trained by regional trainers who were previously trained as part of a train-the-trainer program. All 140 coaches are ready to lead their Learning Groups.

Day 20: The coaches with past experience independently lead their teams through a Launch Workshop using native language. The newly trained coaches co-lead a Launch

Workshop with their regional trainer. The CSRs think that the program was developed just for their region and actively learn the new business processes and culture.

Day 21: The Guided Practicum begins in local language for 1,200 CSRs in 140 Learning Groups.

Month 5: Ninety percent of the CSRs certify as displaying the attitudes and behaviors desired for the new culture.

Step	Process
#1: Wisdom Discovery	Conduct a Wisdom Discovery, ideally with star representatives from all critical business units and/or regions.
#2: Delta Wisdom Discovery	Conduct a Delta Discovery for each business unit or region that requires a custom program.
#3: Phased Deployment (only if you need a new approach)	Decide the optimum sequence of business units and/or regions for deploying the program; don't try to do too much at once.
#4: Local Language (only if using complete local language)	Translate the best practices into the local language.
#5: Combined Launch Workshop and Guided Coaching	Coaches lead the Launch Workshops as a regular Guided Practicum session and flow naturally into the full Guided Practicum.
#6: Certify, Finish, and Sustain	Coaches lead the closure workshop and complete the certification, celebrate success, and if appropriate, continue on to Sustainer.

TABLE 8-2. Six steps for subsequent Affirmative Leadership programs.

Table 8-2 shows the process for launching a second Affirmative Leadership program.

The Discovery sessions are the same, but the decisions about a phased approach and local language are reduced. The train-the-trainer, Leading Group Learning coach training, and Launch Workshop facilitation are eliminated completely. Once the infrastructure is in place, all an organization really needs to do is conduct the Discovery Workshops and put the results into the coaching system. From that point on, the system takes over and anything can be completely and quickly implemented.

This is what happened at MegaChip, and it's happened at many other organizations. Any new initiative or program can go from Discovery to globally scaled in less than two weeks, with minimal expense. The Affirmative Leadership infrastructure enables organizations to achieve the long-desired goal of scaling: extremely effective, fast, and inexpensive Affirmative Leadership for anyone, anywhere, even if there are thousands of potential leaders.

EXPERIENCE A REAL-WORLD EXECUTIVE PROGRAM

SEEING HOW ONE COMPANY CREATED AN EXECUTIVE LEADERSHIP PROGRAM

Tim defines and implements leadership development programs for Comptech, a high-technology manufacturer. When the company's primary business changed from laptop computers to tablets, it was Tim's job to assess the management team's ability to deal with all the changes necessitated by the new market. Tim's analysis showed that only 5 percent of the management team was capable of leading the transformation. He needed to develop many more, and better, leaders fast.

This chapter is a detailed real world example of how Comptech developed those leaders and changed its culture. The reader will see how all of the elements of Affirmative Leadership came together to create great engagement and learning for the executive leadership development candidates and how the real world challenges many programs face can be overcome.

We chose Comptech because its experience is typical of what many companies experience when facing significant market changes that demand better leadership. In particular, the Comptech example shows how executives can and will be active participants in their own development if a program's content and the process are consistent with the participants' self-images as executives.

AN EXISTENTIAL LEADERSHIP CHALLENGE

When tablet computing drastically cut into Comptech's dominance of the server, desktop, and laptop computer market, Comptech executives were shocked. They had scorned tablets as "toys" that could never compete with "real computers," and now tablet sales were growing rapidly while sales of their computers had stalled. Comptech had to become a player in the tablet market.

Comptech's executive team realized that everything about tablets—the technology, sales process, pricing, and delivery channels—was different from their own computers. Tim, a manager responsible for leadership programs, examined Comptech and concluded that it did not have the right people to lead the company into the new market. Comptech needed to do something fast. It needed a leadership development program that would quickly grow a large group of new leaders who could lead the transformations to tablets.

Tim was certain that standard approaches wouldn't work. Affirmative Leadership had a good track record in other parts of the company. With considerable trepidation, he decided to do a very limited, carefully controlled and measured test of Affirmative Leadership. The initial focus was "how to be a great program leader for the product delivery process." He enlisted support for this test up through the executive vice president of operations.

WISDOM DISCOVERY WORKSHOP

To introduce Affirmative Leadership to her learning group, a Comptech coach said, *"This program came from the best of our people. It is all ours, not some outsider's."*

One of the most important elements of Affirmative Leadership for Comptech was that it was entirely homegrown. Comptech's culture was so strong, and its leadership requirements were so specific, that standard approaches to leadership development that relied on formal, research-based models, even when customized, were perceived as irrelevant to Comptech's needs. The content of a leadership development program had to come from internal sources and reflect Comptech's unique situation to be acceptable to the participants.

Since this was leadership for the new markets, Tim used the star selection criteria for "stretch discovery" (the type of discovery used when at least a portion of the core expertise isn't fully known). Tim asked the executive team for a list of ten names of people from operations around the world who were highly respected for their demonstrated ability to lead similar transformations. The nomination process generated a list of ten people averaging twenty-five years of tenure. These ten people were flown to headquarters for a three-day Wisdom Discovery workshop.

OUR STARS' WISDOM

Kevin, the executive sponsor, introduced the program by talking to the group about the market changes and the need for leadership. Lee, the outside facilitator, introduced the Discovery Workshop process. Lee transitioned directly from his presentation into the detective role. With this level of experience in the room, Lee expected the exemplars to be unconsciously competent.

Lee was looking for a definition of the Purpose of being a great manager for the transformation from computers to tablets. He began by trying to get the group to brainstorm about the transformation's goals and what was needed from the program managers to achieve them. He recorded the group's ideas in a computer and projected them on a big screen.

The first items—make money for the company, improve our productivity, and so on—were predictably tactical. The participants were thinking theoretically. After about ten minutes, Lee stopped the brainstorming:

"I know many of you, and I can tell you that this doesn't come close to what makes you stars. Now tell me this: Do you love your jobs?"

In joking language, everyone said they did.

"Why do you love your jobs?"

And the floodgates opened.

Candidates talked intensely about translating strategy to action, influencing the direction of the company, building a high-performing team, solving complex problems, and other exciting motives. Even the stars from Japan, Malaysia, and China, who were often reserved, jumped in when Lee called on them.

When the group had made a good working list of what constituted greatness, Lee transitioned everyone into small groups to create 300-character Purpose statements expressing the core ideas. The small group discussions were intense, with people poking at the computer screens and talking intensely as they wrote their Purpose statements. Lee collected the small group content, and the whole group began to consolidate all the statements into one.

Almost immediately Andy, one of the most senior and highly respected stars, challenged the others by saying that he thought they were doing the wrong program. He said that "great program management" was really "great transformational leadership." He said they needed to do a program about great transformational leadership, not program management.

The stunned silence in the room was quickly followed by an outburst of agreement. Everyone thought that the Discovery program needed to focus on great transformational leadership. Four hours later, they produced this compelling Purpose statement:

As a trusted transformational leader, my passionate commitment and skills enable me to guide creation of a compelling collective vision and empower others to convert the vision to action. I courageously make the hard decisions needed to drive excellent, long-term results.

Excited by their Purpose statement, the group dove into creating their path to mastery (that is, the Big Steps), the major capabilities a transformational leader needs to develop. Working in small groups again, the teams identified and sequenced five major focus areas for development that any potential executive would need to master to be great. The whole group then consolidated the small group work into a list of Big Steps with clear titles and detailed descriptions for each:

- COMPELLING VISION: My authenticity, beliefs, and confidence are the primary drivers for creating purpose for my organization. My superb business acumen enables me to sense unique opportunities and articulate them as a compelling vision that has the potential to produce extraordinary business results.
- DEEP ALIGNMENT: I build a comprehensive network of stakeholders and key influencers based on mutual trust and benefit. My network actively supports the vision by speaking about it positively and frequently and formally allocating needed resources.
- PERFORMANCE INFRASTRUCTURE: I drive efficient organization of the work required to achieve the vision. We establish an effective operating model that includes excellent planning and ongoing management. We are self-consciously great managers of the work and our team.
- TRANSFORMATIONAL CULTURE: I am a model of transformational leadership working to create a culture where everyone embraces change, and greatness is our

goal. I enjoy and encourage others to enjoy "pushing the envelope" of innovation in our products, services, business processes and, most importantly, ourselves.

- SUSTAINED EXTRAORDINARY PERFORMANCE: I build a learning culture in my organization that consistently delivers high performance. We institutionalize our excellence.

As the stars reviewed the Big Steps, a consensus emerged that they would be equally useful to any Comptech executive anywhere and should be used to develop every executive and potential executive in Comptech. This type of expansion is typical of stars because they always think about the larger context and seek to expand perspectives and value.

Much of the deep wisdom comes from digging deeper into the meaning of the Big Steps by specifically defining Mastery. The group quickly plunged into defining the next level of detail, the driving Principles.

Lee created new small-group teams that quickly became deeply engaged in discussions about what it meant to master a particular Big Step. For example, while there was general agreement among the team working on the "compelling vision" Big Step, there was considerable debate about its exact meaning. The team worked hard to define mastery of authenticity and trust, eventually producing the following Principles:

- I am deeply and genuinely committed to creating a greater social good for our clients, my team, and the organization. My authenticity and purpose are the foundation of my transformational leadership.
- I do the homework required to develop superb business acumen, particularly when information is incomplete and trends are uncertain. I seek unique, innovative opportunities that align with our growth strategies.
- I articulate the vision of the opportunity in a compelling

way. Everyone knows that this is worth doing and has a general idea of how it can be achieved.

- I courageously evangelize the vision with conviction, urgency, and a sense of certainty to encourage people to believe in it. I maintain my commitment, even when there is uncertainty and/or when I encounter resistance.

Once the group was satisfied with the Principles they had created, they talked about how they had acquired their own wisdom and knowledge. For example, members of the team working on the compelling vision Big Step said:

- *"The manager led a team through defining what really mattered in a project."*
- *"I got inspiration from the obvious emotional commitment and conviction of a leader."*
- *"I had a sense that you could simply believe the person—they always delivered."*
- *"I spent time reflecting on my own reasons for doing the job."*
- *"I attended a class on vision statements."*
- *"I read* DRiVE *by Dan Pink and* Switch *by Chip and Dan Heath."*

There were many more comments. All of the teams generated similar lists, and they became the foundation for creating the learning program.

In the final section of the Comptech Wisdom Discovery, Lee demonstrated how the best practices developed by the stars would be used in the coaching process to transfer the expertise to leadership development candidates. The stars thought that executives and senior managers should be coaches, and several of them immediately volunteered to coach. The stars' enthusiasm for the best practices and willingness to be coaches were indicative of their strong engagement with and commitment to Affirmative Leadership.

CREATING THE LEARNING EXERCISES

Tim and Lee created a series of very short (less than thirty-minute) exercises that were likely to drive people to think about and/or experience some aspect of the key leadership concepts. Table 9-1 shows some of the Learning Tasks for the Comptech "transformational culture" Big Step.

Driving Principle for Transformational Culture Big Step	Learning Exercise for Each Principle	Supporting Resource
I am a model of transformation by continuously, consciously working hard to improve myself and framing all changes as opportunities for self-improvement.	Write one or two sentences describing what it means for me to be a model of transformational leadership and why modeling is so important. List three behaviors that show I am modeling transformational leadership. Share with a peer. Review the Einstein quote on insanity. List two things I will change about myself and two ways I will lead differently to help create a transformational culture. Write one or two sentences about why I must change before I can expect others to change.	Web address for the Einstein quote on insanity
I treat everyone as a change leader and I expect my team and network to treat all others as change leaders, regardless of position on the organizational chart.	Create a presentation about the value of developing an environment where everyone makes a leadership contribution. List two things I can do to help create a leadership-rich environment.	

TABLE 9-1. Transformational leadership Principles and Tasks.

Learning Group	#1	#2	#3	#4
Coach Base	California	California	California	Singapore
Participants	California only	California only	Global	Global

TABLE 9-2.   Comptech Learning Groups Launch.

The learning tasks for Big Step 4 on transformational culture were less tangible and more sophisticated than earlier Big Steps. As the Comptech leadership candidates went through the program, these learning tasks guided executives and potential executives to apply the Principles to their own organizations, which drove awareness, overcame barriers, and ultimately created transformational cultures.

Tim then began the work required for a pilot test. Comptech executives had to nominate candidates based on their growth potential. Tim formed them into four Learning Groups, including two international groups with participants from the United States, Asia, and Europe. All groups had people from different business units to increase the diversity of perspectives. Tim assigned a coach to each group from the volunteers. He established a schedule for the Leading Group Learning coach training (discussed in the next section) and for the Launch Workshops, including working out the logistics for the international participants (Table 9-2).

LEADING GROUP LEARNING COACH TRAINING

Coaches had to be trained in Leading Group Learning. We were concerned that the executives who would be coaching would resist being trained themselves—even though they had volunteered. Lee trained the American coaches in leading group learning at a central site in California. Jim, another facilitator who was supported by Tim, trained the Singapore coach and a backup Asian coach in two two-and-a-half-hour Web sessions.

In both training sessions, the coaches were immediately engaged by Dan Pink's short video on motivation and the ensuing discussion about the role of "purpose" in leadership. However, they talked about how the candidates would establish purpose for their organizations, but not about their own purpose as coaches. As Randy, one of the coaches in the California training class, put it: *"I didn't expect this to be about me as a coach."* These comments led to an intense discussion about the coach's role as models of learning and how they needed to make sure they were great leaders before they could coach others. The coaches wrote their Purpose statement, shared it with the other coaches, and commented on everyone else's statements. The coaches rapidly became models of the same type of learning they would soon be leading.

As the coaches rolled into the coach's path to Mastery section of the Leading Group Learning coach training, they were shocked to realize that they would have to complete a multi-month program themselves to become great leaders of group learning. Eventually, though, they understood that the new science in the field of coaching held something useful to teach them.

This "not for me" attitude changed completely and permanently when it was time to practice leading a group in how to learn the leadership best practices. None of the coaches could do it. They either talked the entire time about their own ideas or had a series of one-to-one dialogues without any cross talk or group learning. Feedback led to good introspection and a real recognition that they had something to learn. In the second practice exercise, they were much more humble, listening to each other and encouraging cross talk. As Wendy, one of the coaches put it: *"I am so used to being the one who is talking that I am having a hard time just stopping and listening. This is really great leadership training for me."* The coaches realized that they needed to become great leaders themselves in order to teach others to be great leaders, which was a huge revelation to most. It was the start of a valuable development experience.

The day after the coach training classes were completed, we kicked off the Affirmative Leadership program with Launch Workshops co-led by Lee and the local coach for all of the candidates. The two American groups were in a California facility. A mixed American and European group, led by a coach based in the United States, met via video conference in the morning; and the Asian group, led by the coach from Singapore, met at 6:00 PM Pacific time via video conference.

LAUNCH WORKSHOP

Tim and a few of the coaches feared that executive candidates would be very resistant to being led into discussions based on the best practices using the persuasive technology and would not engage sufficiently to develop their attitudes and skills. They also feared that executive candidates were too busy and impatient to do the learning exercises, talk with each other, and record their learnings. These concerns are typical of every executive program we have done.

Tim kicked off both Launch Workshops with a standard Comptech-style PowerPoint presentation about the objectives and history of the program. He then handed off to Lee, the facilitator, who did a short introduction, and he then quickly deferred to the coaches for their introductions. When the coaches introduced the program, the candidates realized something different was about to happen. They leaned forward and seemed to hang on the coach's every word. Later, all said they had never heard their coaches speak that way before. They liked the way the coaches were talking to them, but found it very different.

After the introductions, Lee asked candidates in the Launch Workshop to read the stars' Purpose statement and focus on one idea that stood out for them:

As a trusted transformational leader, my passionate commitment and skills enable me to guide creation of a compelling collective vision and empower others to convert the vision to action. I courageously make the hard decisions needed to drive excellent, long-term results.

This was the first inflection point in the program because it was unclear how the candidates would react. After a brief pause, Robert, one of the candidates in the California session, commented that "courageously making hard decisions" struck him because it was sometimes hard for him to go against conventional wisdom and upper management expectations. Jill, also in the California workshop, chimed in with a comment about how "empowering others" was really talking about accomplishing something through others and not just being a great individual contributor. Similarly, in the Asian workshop, Chin Wu commented on the importance of his own commitment to motivating others, and Makato from Japan talked about the importance of personal commitment to leadership. In all Launch Workshops, the candidates commented on particularly interesting or provocative ideas from the purpose statement. In a matter of minutes, the candidates demonstrated intense engagement.

The engagement intensified when Lee paired people up and asked them to discuss greatness in leadership at Comptech, using the Purpose statement. He also asked them to learn something from their partners and write an anchor. After a brief time, Lee switched the pairs for another discussion of greatness.

Finally, with the coach's leadership, the entire Learning Group discussed greatness. The candidates appeared to be thrilled by the opportunity to discuss their ideas about greatness in CompTech leadership with peers and record their perspectives. They said this was the first time they'd been asked to explicitly think about the meaning of greatness in their roles, and they appreciated the insights they got from each other.

Here are some examples of what they wrote:

Mayumi: *"In Japan, trust of leadership is critical. I must gain trust by being a real person. I mean and do what I say."*

Neal on "compelling collective vision": *"I always thought that I was the one who was supposed to come up with the vision and sell it to others. Jill made me realize that it is actually better for me to guide my group to define the vision together."*

Tom: *"I am a results person, but I can see how when I just focus on results, I am missing the importance of my own energy and excitement to others. I need to both show my commitment and excitement . . . and still get the results."*

Affirmative Leadership for executives had passed a critical test at Comptech. The candidates' engagement was high and the comments were insightful. In addition, norms had been established about using the best practices as the foundation for discussion, the process for recording in the persuasive technology, listening to each other as a source of expertise, and the authority of their coach as the person guiding the learning process.

As the candidates read, discussed, and recorded their thoughts about the focus and importance of each Big Step, the discussions gradually tied more closely to their personal reality, expanded their notions of greatness as they saw the content of the later Big Steps, and drove them toward self-directed learning. For instance, in discussing the "deep alignment" Big Step, Cheryl, who was leading a significant change to Comptech's manufacturing in support of going into the tablet

market, said that *"building my network was critical for my success as a leader because the changes involved an incredible number
of departments and organizations."* She said that she *"kept getting
surprised by concerns from groups that I never thought about, but
that would be directly relevant to my work."* Similarly, Gerry, who
ran logistics and warehouse operations, commented about his
concerns about getting pickers and packers in the warehouse,
who are under constant time pressures to ship the product
needed, to be able to make a bigger contribution to developing
the organization. Subtly, without prompting but with overt
support from their peers in the learning group and their coach,
the candidates applied the concepts from the best practices to
their own situations. In minutes, a theoretical exercise became
personal and practical. and the learning visibly soared.

The Principles themselves and the coaches' questions drove
the candidates to make still more important and critical connections between the concepts presented in the best practices
and their work. For example, the following Principle produced an excellent discussion about what it meant to have
"superb business acumen":

I do the homework required to develop superb business
acumen particularly when information is incomplete and
trends are uncertain. I understand our strategic objectives, study the broader trends in the market, "check the
edge," and talk to many clients (internal and external).

Vanessa, one of the candidates, really struggled with this
one, commenting that her job was to take a strategy and just
get the work done. She didn't believe that she needed business acumen to be a successful leader. Her colleagues began
discussing ways they develop and apply business acumen
and why this is so critical for being a leader. Vanessa said: *"I
have never thought of myself that way, but I can see how I should
focus more on judgments than just work."*

In a different group, Lin, who was in Malaysia, commented that Asian manufacturing and shipping was changing very fast, including a redirection to Brazil. The idea of "checking the edge" about recent trends was a very useful way to describe what she should be doing more regularly. In these discussions, both Vanessa and Lin began to develop some of the perspectives that make someone a great leader. Vanessa moved from executing others' strategies to creating strategies. Lin developed a wider and more strategically important view of her role. The learning was already working.

The process for refining and scheduling the Learning Tasks further stretched candidates' perceptions. They were expected to understand the overall thrust of the learning task and adapt it to create intense value. This caused some consternation in the Learning Groups. They were so used to having assignments given to them, and were so good at executing them, that the idea of interpreting and changing a task to make it work best for them was a very foreign notion. The coaches told them that the only boundaries were that their adjustments needed to be consistent with the task's intent, the time available for it, and their conviction that the learning would be valuable. It was challenging for the candidates to move this far into self-directed learning this fast.

However, after one or two tasks, they all got the idea and raced ahead, led by their coaches. For example, this is how one Learning Group processed Big Step 1, learning task 8:

Identify two people outside of Comptech who are great at telling a compelling story (for example, the Kennedy moonshot speech). Describe the characteristics of a great story.

The Learning Group realized that being able to tell a compelling story would improve their abilities to articulate their Purpose. They liked the idea of using something outside of their business as an example, but also thought they needed something related directly to Comptech—so they modified the assignment. Some participants were to bring outside examples while others were to bring Comptech examples. By this time, coaches and group participants were completely engaged. The Comptech candidates were self-directed learners and were becoming Affirmative Leaders.

In the final module the coaches guided the candidates into deeper reflective learning by having each candidate record two or three key learnings from the Launch Workshop in the persuasive technology and share their key learnings with the others in the group:

> Chin Wu: *"I learned that the Bangalore team has many of the same issues as I have in Singapore. I always thought they were different but a lot of the leadership challenges are the same."*
>
> Gerry: *"I learned that I am responsible for better connecting the work of the organization to our strategy. I had been leaving this pretty much to chance. I need to get clearer about my purpose, our purpose, and the value it creates."*
>
> Tom: *"I love the learning process. I already learned a lot from my peers in my learning group. It is a really great way to learn. It fits my style well."*

The Affirmative Leadership Launch Workshop for Comptech executives began to change their paradigm into self-directed learning around the real complexities and realities of leadership in today's organizations. Both the coaches and candidates knew that something different and powerful was going on.

GUIDED PRACTICUM

Each week, led by their coaches, the Learning Groups used the Do-Discuss-Anchor cyclical pattern to expand, apply, and reflect on their learnings. What follows is how one Comptech leadership Learning Group went through this cycle. Returning to the Learning Task 8 discussed earlier (the one about finding great stories), here is a sampling of what individuals brought into the group:

Sue (responsible for tablet marketing) brought in Steve Job's introduction of the iPhone and a presentation by the CEO of ARM Technology, a significant driver of the tablet market, because she saw these as directly related to the marketing she would be doing in the future.

Gerry (responsible for European logistics) brought in the speech by General George Patton to the U.S. Third Army during the Battle of the Bulge in World War II and a presentation by the CEO of Federal Express because these were directly tied to logistics issues.

Neal (responsible for changing the manufacturing platform to support tablets) used the Kennedy moonshot speech and brought in a speech by Comptech's CEO about the tablet market because these were both about motivating a huge engineering effort.

Each candidate presented their examples and analysis of what made the stories great (or not so great). As a group they agreed that great motivational stories convey the storyteller's passion and include:

- A compelling description of achieving a significant social good (that is, a purpose)
- The benefits of achieving the social good to individuals, organizations, and/or society
- How the social good could be achieved
- A call for action

Again without prompting, the discussion moved toward how well they were doing these things when presenting to their teams. They were naturally starting to work on key leadership visioning and communication skills. Here is what they recorded as their learnings:

> Sue: *"Being passionate and having all four elements is critical because they complement each other and create a holism of purpose and action. If anything gets left out, there is a real gap in what people need to know to be motivated and to act. I have been focusing too much on the glory of the social good and not enough on how to get there or the call to action."*
>
> Gerry: *"I am such an analytic nerd sometimes. I never really thought about the passion and purpose aspects. I always just thought you told people what to do and they would go and do it. Now I see that each of these elements plays a very important role in leading a group. It makes me a little uncomfortable to talk about passion and purpose, but I guess that is why I am in this class. I do love what we are doing. I have to show it more."*
>
> Neal: *"I love the idea of a story instead of a mission statement. Stories have so much more life and energy. Our mission statements are pretty lame, mostly about the how to do a task or project without any real information about why we should do it. I think a story would be fun to tell which is different from my endless presentation of a boring mission statement."*

The candidates were already well into task 9 before they formally started it:

Create a "story" around my purpose and share it with a safe peer. Be sure it is compelling. Ask specifically for feedback on my passion, logic, tie to Comptech strategy, and value created. Modify as needed.

As a result of task 8, the groups were already thinking about their own presentations, but moving to actually creating stories was a significant, and for many, a very scary move forward. This was no longer a theoretical exercise, but required specific, perhaps risky, action.

The group then discussed what it meant to present to a "safe peer" and modified the task to include telling their stories to each other before telling them to anyone outside the group. They committed to having their stories done in three days, arranged to present to each other in pairs within two days, and finish presenting to a safe peer before the next group learning meeting. The coach asked them if they wanted to take on this much work, and their immediate response was: *"This is really useful. It is not extra work. It is what I am supposed to do."*

A week later they reported that they were all surprised by how well the learning exercise had worked and how favorably their presentations had been received. Everyone said showing passion and focusing on purpose made a huge difference to the attention paid to the message and quality of the response. Several people said that their safe peers had found their stories really great.

Almost everyone's confidence blossomed, so much that people outside the program commented on the change. For example, shortly before the weekly debriefing meeting, Neal's manager sent this e-mail to the coach: *"What did you do with Neal? He is so much more confident and articulate. He gave a great, incredibly motivating presentation to our group. Good work."*

The ongoing coach's meetings and use of the persuasive technology provided Tim, the coaches, the facilitator, and management with valuable information about the candidates' progress. Coaches could see exactly what their candidates were recording, evaluate the quality of the learning, and, if necessary, guide the candidates to improve. For example, Tim noticed Randy's group falling behind, met with Randy to examine the causes, and immediately escalated the matter to the candidates' managers to keep the focus on the program. Tim also used the technology's capability to print reports of specific learnings to keep the candidates' managers and the executive sponsor informed. This infrastructure made it easier for Tim to justify the value of the program.

In the ensuing Big Steps the demands on the candidates increased dramatically. For example, Big Step 4, transformational culture, took the learnings from all of the previous Big Steps to a new level. As Tom put it, *"As I did this task, I realized that I was already thinking and acting more like a transformational leader, but I need to be more conscious of how I show it."* Working in small increments, the Comptech candidates had now done everything in their objective statement, including the very last phrase, "drive excellent long-term results." Every candidate was now a great transformational leader.

REAL LEADERSHIP IMPACT

The last task in the entire program was for the candidates and the coaches to review all of their recorded learnings, which were considerable (Cheryl had forty-two pages of learnings) and prepare a presentation about three or four that they found most relevant to their development as leaders. The teams presented their key learnings and evaluated the learning process in a formal closure session.

The key learnings that emerged were mainly about the intangibles. Here is a sample:

- My personal passion and commitment is the single most important factor in leading others.
- I am always balancing conflicting pressures like being both transactional and transformation, driving performance and empowering, thinking short-term but laying the foundation for the long-term.
- I must provide time and safe opportunity for my people to think and reflect, as these are the most important elements in growth.
- I must produce results or we will fail as an organization.

- The coaches got more from the sessions than the candidates (and the candidates got a lot).

Shortly after this, Tim completed the final certification-lite survey of the candidates, their managers, their peers, and the coaches (Table 9-3).

While the candidates improved in all areas, the attitudes and skills associated with compelling vision and transformational culture improved the most. Many had thought that the intangibles could only be learned from years of experience, yet they learned them in six months. Finally, all of the coaches and most of the managers recommended the program at the highest possible level (4.8 rounded off to 5). It was widely thought that this program had far exceeded the original expectations for preparing deeper transformational leadership for the transition to tablets by also generally increasing the depth and quality of Comptech's leadership.

The most important indicators of success were that the executive team made the program mandatory for all executives—

Big Step and Description	Pre-Average Score	Post-Average Score
COMPELLING VISION	3.2	4.5
DEEP ALIGNMENT	3.1	4.3
PERFORMANCE INFRASTRUCTURE	4.1	4.6
TRANSFORMATIONAL CULTURE	1.6	4.2
SUSTAINED EXTRAORDINARY PERFORMANCE	3.2	4.2
Would you recommend this program to others? (only given to candidates, their managers, and the coaches)		4.8

TABLE 9-3. Certification-lite scores.

vice presidents, directors, and potential directors—and all of the Learning Groups decided to continue to meet. Not only did the candidates internalize the learnings, but Comptech now had a consistent, reliable process for developing and sustaining great Affirmative Leaders.

UNLEASH THE SUPPRESSED ENERGY OF FRONTLINE MANAGERS

TRANSFORMING TRANSACTIONAL FRONTLINE MANAGERS INTO INSPIRING LEADERS

Jason hates the words, *"he filed a grievance with his union rep against his frontline manager* (FLM)," because Jason is responsible for reducing union complaints. He is the human resources manager for LocalPower, a mid-sized electrical public utility, and is responsible for developing leadership programs that minimize union complaints, most of which are about FLMs. Jason has to teach FLMs to walk a fine line between the sometimes conflicting demands of their organization, such as ensuring a fast response to a power outage, and the union requirements, which might, for example, restrict who is allowed to respond to the outage. Jason uses Affirmative Leadership to develop FLMs that collaborate well with and are actually liked by the union representatives.

Organizations are increasingly aware of the importance of FLMs as the glue that connects the work of an organization to its strategy. Being an FLM is a particularly challenging role because FLMs must simultaneously accomplish all of the daily work of an organization while transforming their teams into increasingly high performers. FLM leadership programs, developed and implemented using the Affirmative Leadership model, convert highly transactional managers into great transformational leaders without sacrificing operational excellence.

In this chapter you will experience two very different Affirmative Leadership programs for FLMs—one at LocalPower, a challenging, unionized public utility, and the other from DigiAd, a fast-paced advertising sales organization. It provides the reader with insight into how to develop and implement an FLM program and presents the real challenges FLMs face in trying to develop their capabilities, including a strike in the middle of the LocalPower program and a declaration of Chapter 11 bankruptcy during the DigiAd sales program. These two examples of FLM programs were selected because they highlight commonalities in all FLM programs as well as the subtle modifications to FLM Affirmative Leadership programs required to accommodate unique differences in any environment.

A CHALLENGING ROLE

FLMs (or their many equivalents such as team leaders, store/restaurant managers, and project managers—anyone who is responsible for guiding the work of individual contributors) are the ligaments and tendons of organizations. FLMs are expected to connect the work of the organization to its strategy, to be able to perform the technical work of the group and be its leader, to make daily numbers while building for the future, and to give credit to the team without expecting credit for building the team. The FLM role can be very challenging and stressful.

Fortunately, there are star FLMs who thrive in the role by being transformational leaders in a way that effectively manages all of these conflicting pressures and consistently produces transactional excellence. We are going to follow two Affirmative Leadership programs for FLMs—in a sales environment at DigiAd and in an electric public utility,

LocalPower—to learn how they accomplish this challenging synthesis.

DigiAd was the fifth largest seller of yellow page advertising in the country, selling $800 million of ads each year to help local businesses generate leads. Unfortunately for DigiAd, ad sales were declining at 20 percent per year, so it was only a matter of time, and not much time, before the company was out of business. DigiAd executives realized this and were determined to convert from print-only to "selling integrated print and digital solutions." More specifically, they decided to expand from print-only yellow page ads to ads in commercial websites, videos, and search sites such as Google, Bing, and Yahoo. In order to make this change, DigiAd had to keep its current revenue from selling print ads *and* convert the entire company to selling the digital ads.

This required changing every aspect of the company including product and solution knowledge, sales processes, and business processes (for example, how to place an order). While all of the company was affected, the sales team leaders (STLs), who managed teams of four to fifteen sales representatives, were the most critical to the transition because they had to connect the corporate strategy to the generation of sales. Either the STLs succeeded in being simultaneously transformational and transactional or the company went under.

LocalPower, while not in such a dire situation as DigiAd, also had significant challenges. The public expected that LocalPower would supply power no matter what, and so even a small failure, such as a transformer exploding and causing a power failure for a few hundred homes, became a performance and public relations disaster. In addition, while its own power generation—coal and oil—was tightly regulated, its competitors—solar and wind—were subject to a lot less regulation. This was lowering what LocalPower could charge for its power, threatening current and future revenues. As if all this wasn't enough, LocalPower's workers were unionized and an increasingly hostile relationship had developed between the company's executives and the union.

The LocalPower FLMs were at the center of these pressures. Distrust of the company usually surfaced as formal union complaints against FLMs, but FLMs were frequently caught in terrible situations. The union agreement, for instance, said that only those in certain job categories could fix an exploding transformer, but once when a transformer was about to explode, no one in that job category was available. So Mala, the FLM responsible for fixing the transformer, had only a few choices—all of them bad. Her options were to:

- Delay the work until someone was available (which would bring down the wrath of LocalPower executives and result in reduced compensation because of missing response time targets)
- Do the work herself (probably triggering a union complaint)
- Have someone other than from the approved job category do the work (also probably triggering a union complaint)
- Authorize overtime (which would violate LocalPower financial guidelines)
- Work with a hostile union shop steward to find a solution (which required significant political and social skills)

Mala was at the center of an incredibly difficult situation. FLMs at LocalPower were expected to prevent problems and resolve them fast if they did arise, but Mala (like many FLMs in similar situations) had no good ways to do either.

WISDOM DISCOVERY

Wisdom Discovery for FLM Affirmative Leadership programs has some particular challenges. First, it is often more difficult to identify FLM stars than senior managers or executives. There is greater resistance to giving those who are identified the time to participate, and FLMs tend to be less articulate about their roles than people higher on the organizational change, thus requiring additional probing by the facilitator. On the other hand, once a group of star FLMs breaks through to talking openly about how they really think and what they actually do to make difficult situations consistently successful, there is a release of energy that is quite astounding to them and to others, including their bosses.

During the process of identifying star FLMs, both DigiAd and LocalPower confused scoring high on metrics with being a star. At DigiAd, the initial executive response was to name people who consistently performed the best on sales metrics. However, these STLs often failed the respect tests because they achieved their performance by driving their teams so hard for short-term performance that they didn't satisfy customers or staff. They made their numbers, but customers and employees did not like to work with or for them.

DigiAd executives eventually came to a more balanced view of stars. The FLMs they chose certainly had to have shown that they could drive the numbers, but their behavior needed to be consistent with core cultural values about respecting others and the need to transform the organization. The final list of DigiAd stars was of people who truly represented the best of DigiAd values and STL skills both in quantitative and, more importantly, qualitative perspectives.

LocalPower had similar issues with metrics, but in an even more challenging way. LocalPower wanted an FLM program that spanned diverse organizational units such as power generation, field service and repair, billing, and power transmission. LocalPower also started with metrics such as response time to outages or costs of generating power, but quickly discovered that metrics didn't reveal much about group dynamics within or across groups.

An FLM who was good at his craft but not at leading a team or working with other departments couldn't model team leadership or interdepartmental cooperation and integration. LocalPower chose good team leaders who were also highly respected by those in other disciplines. Identifying stars made LocalPower's management refine their ideas about greatness in the organization. They selected FLMs who represented the best of what the executives wanted LocalPower to become.

At both DigiAd and LocalPower, the FLMs were very nervous about participating in a workshop in which they'd have to talk a lot. They also were leery of doing anything too intellectual and being too visible to executives. LocalPower FLMs, whose skills were functional (for example, stringing high-voltage wires), especially worried about public speaking and learning about leadership conceptually. As Walter, one of the LocalPower FLMs put it, "*We are action people. We fix broken machines and don't like to sit around and talk. We never talk with executives.*"

Few of the LocalPower FLMs were used to speaking in public. Some were not native English speakers. There was considerable concern about the possible demands of the Wisdom Discovery Workshop.

While the STLs at DigiAd had all come from sales and were more verbal, they also indicated that three days of intellectual discussion, some of which would be observed by senior management, was a sharp departure from their norm. They were used to being out and about with fast-changing groups of teams and customers. While they were intrigued by the idea of talking about greatness with their peers, they were uncomfortable with the format. It just seemed like too much talk and too much exposure.

At DigiAd, in order to put people at ease, the facilitator quickly reached the question: "*Do you love your work?*" None of them had ever been asked that before and they all stopped talking to reflect. Gradually, they answered "yes."

When the facilitator said, *"Why do you love your work?"* the floodgates opened and all resistance fell away. Talking about why they loved their work was both tangible and exciting. As Sheila, a DigiAd STL, put it, *"I never thought of myself that way, but just talking about why I love doing this and how I can be great is, well—great."*

To them, the work they loved was making their numbers, inspiring their people, helping them generate more leads, and empathizing with their customers. The DigiAd group saw greatness as modeling enthusiasm, working with customer service and billing, understanding the new digital products, and many other qualities. Their list covered three full pages.

Workers at LocalPower were more surprised by the question because it was so different. They did tactical, hands-on work, but they loved what they did, too. They loved doing something critical for their community. They reveled in the technical prowess and problem-solving skills they needed to do it, and the good spirit of a tightly integrated team. They weren't as enthusiastic about dealing well with other departments, managing union relationships, and maintaining a very safe workplace, but they believed these were critical parts of being a great FLM. Their list covered four full pages.

After they went through the process of consolidating their brainstormed lists into a specific objective for being a great FLM, each group produced its results (Table 10-1).

These statements come from drastically different environments, but share a strong sense of energy, commitment to the organization, and enjoyment of being a great FLM. When the LocalPower FLMs read their statements, most changed their view of the program. Derek, a very experienced and respected FLM, commented that they had not used "management" or "manager" anywhere and said, *"Maybe this program is really about leadership, not management."* An intense discussion ensued about the difference; the group concluded that management was too much about administration and

DigiAd	LocalPower
I am privileged to be a passionate leader who champions excellence with integrity. I drive results by building a high-performing, customer-centric team that exceeds objectives regardless of circumstance. I am a role model of integrated customer centricity and performance, building a culture of sales greatness.	As a respected leader, I own and take pride in keeping the lights on. My high energy, commitment to excellence, and composure in difficult situations motivate my team. I create a great place to work where we produce positive results.

TABLE 10-1. FLM objective statements.

not enough about motivating and developing their people. The stars turned to Jason, an HR representative, and asked if they could rename the program "How to Be a Great Frontline Leader"; Jason was thrilled. That was exactly what he had hoped would happen. Because of this new focus on leadership versus management, the FLMs at LocalPower came to be known as FLLs (frontline leaders).

As the teams started the Big Steps, excitement and engagement soared. At both DigiAd and LocalPower, the stars began to see the value of talking with their peers about greatness. At LocalPower, people in different departments rarely talked to each other. During the workshop, the participants had to understand each other's perspectives, integrate them with their own, and produce a common set of Big Steps. Comments like this one by Simon from LocalPower, an FLL in field operations and maintenance, were typical: *"I never knew you did that* (referring to how billing issues got resolved before a service call). *That really explains why I sometimes get a good response and sometimes run into real hostility."* The interdepartmental discussions drove better understanding of the best model of FLL performance.

At DigiAd, all of the salespeople had the same core function, but came from different regions: from Alaska and Hawaii to Florida and Maine. Their sharing was about how differences in the local markets required adaptations, which illuminated better ways to be customer-centric. For example, Kevin told how important websites to support seasonal tourist planning were in Alaska, and how this required enticing displays for non-Alaskans and tight timelines. While relationships were important, fast results were the drivers of a sale. In contrast, Elizabeth from Dayton, Ohio, said they had more of a year-round business based on establishing substantive, friendly relations and creating deeper long-term penetration in the market. As the stars discussed their different markets, they gained a more comprehensive understanding of the total optimum sales process, and the best Big Steps emerged. Table 10-2 shows the Big Steps each organization produced.

Each organization defines the Big Steps differently, but all FLM programs tend to have a similar structure. The sequence goes from more basic to increasingly complex and sophisticated, and it is easy to image the capabilities being developed in each Big Step and as a cumulative impact for all of the Big Steps. As the stars transitioned to defining the Principles, the differentiation between FLM programs became more pronounced since the Principles represent the specific expertise of the stars in their particular discipline and organization. This is the real source of their applied wisdom.

Both the DigiAd and LocalPower stars worked hard to make the Principles very realistic and meaningful for their function, even when there were significant subtleties and challenges to reconciling conflicting pressures. For example, at LocalPower, there was an intense discussion about the Principles associated with the collective bargaining agreement (CBA) between management and the union. The situation with Mala and the exploding transformer and her

DigiAd	LocalPower
PASSIONATE CUSTOMER CENTRICITY: I am deeply committed to customer centricity and develop a team that lives great customer service. We consistently make our numbers with integrity, positive attitude, and team support.	KEEP THE LIGHTS ON: I am fully aligned with our company's foundational values. I am accountable for my personal and team success, improving upon our legacy. I value my team and am committed to serving customers and the community.
SUPERB SOLUTIONS: I embrace our product offerings and can effectively combine them into innovative solutions that meet customer requirements and exceed their expectations.	FUNCTIONAL JOB KNOWLEDGE: I have the functional job knowledge that enables me to ask the right questions and guide my group.
EFFICIENT BUSINESS/SALES PROCESSES: I effectively utilize sales and business management best practices and model excellent sales processes. I manage the qualitative and quantitative aspects of excellent selling processes including setting attainable targets within the context of our business goals.	EFFECTIVE ADMINISTRATION: I understand and am effective at performing all of the administrative functions of the frontline leader. I keep us in compliance with the company's policies and procedures. This keeps us healthy and safe.
HIGH-PERFORMING TEAM: I create a winning environment where all sales representatives feel empowered to make critical, timely decisions. We are a close-knit, mutually supportive team that meets goals and has a good time.	LEAD MY TEAM: I build a high-performing team that is aligned with our company's values and strategic initiatives. I am trusted by my team and lead by example, creating a positive environment where everyone knows what is expected and works together to produce great results.

DigiAd	LocalPower
ORGANIZATION INFLUENCER: I am a voice to the customer and a voice for the customer to the organization. I draw on resources that optimize my direct team's performance and add value to others that improves their performance.	BUILD BRIDGES: I enhance and promote working relationships with other departments within the company to get things done. I build a network that allows me to leverage outside resources.
SALES GREATNESS CULTURE: I am a role model of our best values and processes, interacting with our customers (including the "C" level), and community to build credibility and develop long-term business. I create a culture in which everyone is a transformational leader and achieves transactional excellence.	SUSTAINABILITY: I keep up with and use new technology to improve work procedures. I periodically evaluate work methods and cost efficiencies and am not afraid to make changes to raise the bar.

TABLE 10-2. FLM Big Steps.

restricted choices was discussed as an example of the correct Principle about the CBA and its impact on their decisions. Initially, the stars wrote a Principle that interpreted the CBA in flexible ways that encouraged Mala to work with her union shop steward to allow her to assign someone from an unapproved job category to fix the transformer. While this was a technical violation of the CBA, it was done in conjunction with the union rep and so was considered to be acceptable to the FLLs because it maintained the spirit of the CBA. It was not, however, acceptable to the human resources and legal departments, who required strict official adherence to the CBA. The end result was a Principle that talked about the gray areas in the CBA (Table 10-3) that were acceptable to everyone and related to Principles in other Big Steps about the importance of building good relationships with union shop stewards. Legal considerations prevented the star FLLs from giving direct advice about the union relationship, but they found a way to convey their wisdom about how to handle it.

DigiAd encountered an even more challenging situation around the Principles for account prioritization for their sales reps. DigiAd had hired expensive outside consultants to create a mathematical formula that would analyze all current and potential accounts in the sales database and identify the highest priority accounts. This prioritization algorithm was meant to assign accounts to each sales representative. As the star STLs looked at creating a Principle for using this formula to allocate their accounts, they realized that the formula was incorrect because it seriously undervalued the largest current accounts. When they asked for clarification from Kathy, the vice president responsible for the consultant's work, they were told that the formula could not possibly be incorrect since they had paid millions to the consultants to create it. Stymied by Kathy's response, the stars decided to write two Principles: one saying that STLs should use the formula as it was currently defined and another indicating how they should extend it to address the incorrect focus it created. Ultimately, they proved that the consultants had got it wrong, which was embarrassing for the executives, but satisfying and vindicating for the stars.

These two instances are typical of how crafting realistic Principles helps FLMs cope with their often messy realities. Table 10-3 shows excerpts from the Principles for the fifth Big Step for both companies.

In both cases, the star FLMs were surprised that being an influencer was part of being a great FLM. They'd had a much more narrowly defined view of the FLM role and now were

DigiAd	LocalPower
ORGANIZATION INFLUENCER	BUILD BRIDGES
• I am a voice to the customer and a voice for the customer to the organization. • I proactively expand my personal and my sales team's networks to include other sales representatives and sales team leads in the region, customer service, corporate marketing and product division planning. • I am a role model of the best of everything in our organization to the customer. The customer knows that I speak with the best intent and a great ability to coordinate diverse support, including technical and billing, to provide them with a great experience with us. • I provide other departments with excellent information about our customer's needs and expectations. I am a trusted contributor to their success.	• I enhance and promote working relationships with other departments within the company to get things done. I build a network that allows me to leverage outside resources. • I understand the importance of working relationships with other departments. I build these relationships by offering them my best effort and expect the same. I proactively establish relationships with outside contacts (for example, EPRI, vendors, and so on) that allow me to bring in the resources that are not available internally but are required to complete tasks.

(continued on page 184)

TABLE 10-3.   FLM Principles.

DigiAd	LocalPower
ORGANIZATION INFLUENCER	BUILD BRIDGES
• I see myself as a leader of the organization, regardless of where I am on the formal organization chart. I realize that leadership is about influencing others to be customer-centric and support my personal and my team's efforts. • I systematically develop trusting relationships across the organization based on reliability, caring, and mutual benefit with critical related functions.	• I build a library of learning resources that I can use to improve work methods, techniques, and strategies.

TABLE 10-3. FLM Principles.

recognizing how much larger and more influential their roles actually were. The Learning Tasks associated with Principles were designed to systematically drive the FLMs out of their comfort zones with new responsibilities and new ways of thinking about their roles. For example, for DigiAd's fifth Big Step, "Organization Influencer," the fifth Principle was:

I see myself as a leader of the organization, regardless of where I am on the formal organization chart. I realize that leadership is about influencing others to be customer-centric and support my personal and my team's efforts.

Two of the associated learning tasks were:

• Review the video on influencing. Identify someone who is influential and describe three reasons they are influential. List three things I can do that would make me more influential.

- Identify the departments that are most important to my success. Contact someone in those departments and meet with them to discuss their perceptions of my role. Identify two ways I can help them. Ask for two things they could do to help me.

In the first Learning Task, the STL was guided to reflect on influencing in general, then on his own ability to influence. In the second task, he was guided through listening, finding ways to add value to the other department, and exerting some influence in support of his department. With relatively little effort, the design of the Learning Task guides a learner to reflect on and practice key intangible leadership behaviors: influencing and interdepartmental integration.

SELECTING AND TRAINING COACHES

The different approaches DigiAd and LocalPower took to selecting their coaches illustrate the options and challenges of launching Affirmative Leadership programs.

DigiAd saw the STL development program as a core function of the organization and required the STL's direct managers, the regional managers, to coach their STLs. Using regional managers as coaches reduced potential conflicts with other priorities, and developing their STLs was already a formal part of the regional manager's role. Still, most regional managers believed that "coaching" was making the numbers because the coaching caused the STLs to work harder and drive their sales representatives more aggressively. As a result, many of the regional managers didn't see a need to be trained as coaches, or even to proactively support the customer centricity initiative. When it became apparent that the regional managers' resistance was a significant barrier to the DigiAd transformation, the executive team took a strong stand. Scott, the DigiAd CEO, made the situation very clear to the regional managers:

"We have spent years developing the customer centricity strategy and months evaluating the Affirmative Leadership program. Customer centricity is our future. Affirmative Leadership for sales team leaders is the way we are going to make it happen. Either you are with this program and going to be active, great coaches for the sales team leaders or you are in the wrong job and the wrong company."

Two of the eleven regional managers left the company. The remaining nine were completely committed to coaching the STLs.

LocalPower decided to use experienced trainers from the human resources department as coaches. They wanted to mix learning groups across departments to build a foundation of better relationships among them, and few of the department managers were willing to be coaches. However, using trainers as coaches meant that the department managers were less involved and were likely to pull their FLLs out of development work to support other department needs. As a preventive measure, Jason had the department managers sign a formal "promise and commit" statement, pledging to support the program and schedule monthly update meetings with the coach to give them a status report and reinforce department manager support.

The Leading Group Learning course was also quite different at each company. At LocalPower, the trainers got it in seconds and were focused on learning the specific techniques. They asked many great questions. The only issue was slowing them down enough to be sure they absorbed everything.

At DigiAd, even though Scott had made his and the organization's values, commitment, and expectations very clear, the regional managers didn't like being taught how to lead a Learning Group. They had trouble seeing that the training was for them and that they needed to be role models. Only after considerable discussion did Tony, one of the most influential regional managers, say: *"This training is for us. We need to show people what it means to lead by leading and learning ourselves. Nothing less than our full commitment to developing ourselves first, then our team leaders, will make this work."* The change in the other ten regional managers' attitude was immediate and complete.

LAUNCH WORKSHOP AND GUIDED PRACTICUM

While there was some concern about the willingness of the FLMs to openly discuss crucial management issues, the Launch Workshops generally went smoothly, even though they involved people from several remote locations. DigiAd had eleven Launch Workshops spread from Alaska to Hawaii to Georgia. LocalPower's Launch Workshops were in seven locations that included a room about the size of a small closet, several local hotel conference rooms, and a room overlooking a warehouse. Overall, the launch and follow-through for Big Steps 1, 2, and 3 went as expected. The teams were adjusting the learning tasks to make them practical and effective, doing the learning tasks, meeting to discuss the results, and recording their learning. At LocalPower, for instance, learning tasks about technical knowledge were adapted to apply to transmission operations or power generation as appropriate, and at DigiAd the FLMs were modifying account prioritization to reflect the differences between an urban Seattle market and a rural North Carolina market. Engagement and morale were high.

Then—wham! Major unexpected disruptions hit both organizations. DigiAd declared Chapter 11 bankruptcy, and the LocalPower union went out on strike.

DigiAd went bankrupt because it had borrowed heavily to finance the conversion to the digital offerings and its cash flow was not sufficient to maintain liquidity. DigiAd simply ran out of money. The bankruptcy caused significant angst in the organization, seriously reducing morale in the sales force, which undercut the motivation to sell. The executive team focused on the STLs as the best means of stabilizing the sales force and decided that continuing the Affirmative Leadership program was the best way to help the STLs manage all of the pressures.

The need to lead through the bankruptcy caused only a few slight changes to the DigiAd Affirmative Leadership process for FLMs. First, because new information was coming out of headquarters frequently and rumors were circulating even more frequently, a more effective means of communication with the sales organization had to be found. Coach support meetings of the regional managers, led by the human resources department, were made weekly for more frequent, structured communication. The coaches expanded the STLs' weekly debriefing time to include an update on the bankruptcy and its impact. Third, the coaches became more aggressive at driving the STLs to adapt the weekly learning tasks to directly address the issues caused by the bankruptcy. The Affirmative Leadership process was simultaneously teaching the STLs critical leadership skills and leading the organization through an incredibly challenging disruption.

Similarly, LocalPower's management and union had been negotiating for months and everyone thought they were close to an agreement, but LocalPower's executives wanted to increase the retirement age one year. In many professions, that wouldn't be a significant change, but for someone who is climbing power poles in bad weather, that additional year can be very dangerous. Neither side would give in, so the union called a strike. The impact of the strike on the FLLs was that they had to work incredibly long hours to perform the craft functions needed to keep the power on. The executive team decided to temporarily shut down the Affirmative Leadership program because the FLLs were needed to do the craft work and there weren't any teams to manage anyway.

Eight weeks later, management and the union settled the strike and the union returned to work. But hostility toward the FLLs was significant. The FLLs, who had formerly been colleagues and friends with their union workers, were perceived as siding with management by crossing the picket lines to work, and that was a serious breach of trust. Like DigiAd, the LocalPower executive team saw the Affirmative Leadership program for their FLLs as a means of managing some of the tension and conflict, but first they had to restart the program.

During the eight-week hiatus, the program lost momentum and needed to be reenergized. Jason took the lead by crafting and leading a restart session that included the following:

- Reviewing all of the recorded learnings from the past Big Steps
- Listing three things they would add to or change about the learnings as a result of the strike
- Presenting their new learnings to the learning group
- Reviewing Big Step 4, "LEAD MY TEAM Principles and Tasks"
- Preparing to modify the tasks to reflect the pressures caused by the strike

The FLLs had some difficulty shifting back into a learning mode after the chaos of the strike, but realized that this was an opportunity to discuss the strike, their conflicted position, and strategies for leading a recovery. Initially tepid discussions soon became impassioned statements about the need for recovery and peace.

Fortunately, the next Big Step was "Lead My Team," and

most of the Principles could apply directly to recovering from the strike. Principles such as the following one still clearly applied to the situation and were even more important than before the strike:

> I build a high-performing team that is focused, creative, energetic, positive, and works well together. We push each other by communicating, sharing ideas, and supporting each other for a common goal. We ensure that our company is successful in meeting our safety, operational, and financial goals.

The associated learning tasks required adaptation to the realities of the strike but were a good place to start the discussion. For example, one learning task was to "solicit ideas from the team about three ways that we can build morale and increase bonding. As appropriate, conduct the activities."

As with DigiAd, the FLL meetings became a way to both teach leadership and recover from a major setback.

RESULTS

Even with all of the disruption, DigiAd's sales of digital offerings doubled during the program. While this was due to many factors, most of the executives and all of the regional managers attributed the success to the stability and continuity provided by the structure of the program's weekly meetings. Adapting the expert content to apply to the challenging conditions of the bankruptcy and using the weekly meetings to discuss how the adaptations worked were particularly stabilizing. As Dale, one of the regional managers, put it: *"In the midst of chaos, we had both the best practices, which still really applied, and our weekly meetings. People could count on the program and knew that they had a good sense of direction and support. The program was an island of sanity in a crazy environment."*

At LocalPower, the results were surprisingly positive. Virtually everyone indicated that the return to normal went faster than expected because of the Affirmative Leadership program. The FLLs' managers and the FLLs said the Affirmative Leadership program was an excellent support mechanism that focused their attention on the real issues of recovery. As Harry, one of the FLLs, said: *"Our weekly meetings were a place where we could talk about the morale in our groups and how we might address some of the issues. It was amazing how often that week's learning task would be directly applicable to a problem we were having."*

Most importantly, the union members indicated that the FLLs did a good job of leading the recovery. As Walter, one of the union workers, put it: *"We are a really tough group and we were pretty f . . . ing angry. Danny (his FLL) did a great job of letting us vent, then gradually getting us back into feeling pride for our work. When I look back, I am amazed at how quickly we got back into the routine, and maybe even a little more."*

Perhaps the most important indicator of the effectiveness of the program was that most of the learning groups in both companies asked to continue meeting indefinitely. The groups had formed such a strong and useful bond, and valued the process so much, that they wanted to continue it, even though the Affirmative Leadership programs were officially over. The FLMs had bought into their own development and leadership capability to a phenomenal degree, even though the circumstances were very adverse. The now unsuppressed energy of the FLMs helped their organizations through significant trauma and gave each of them an amazing confidence on their leadership ability.

CONCLUSION

These examples of Affirmative Leadership programs for FLMs illustrate the importance of the FLM's role and the opportunity organizations have to add capabilities. The FLMs at DigiAd and LocalPower grew their capabilities despite terrible situations and provided extraordinary leadership throughout. We chose these two examples because they are such strong examples of the value of Affirmative Leadership, but Affirmative Leadership programs for FLMs have been successfully developed and implemented for diverse roles such as store manager, restaurant manager, pod coach, call center supervisor, manufacturing supervisor, project manager, and many other similar functions (see Chapters 2 to 8). The FLMs at DigiAd and LocalPower became as good as the very best. That can happen at any organization.

DRIVE CULTURAL CHANGE WITH INDIVIDUAL CONTRIBUTOR GRASSROOTS LEADERSHIP

TURNING ISOLATED INDIVIDUAL CONTRIBUTORS INTO INFLUENTIAL LEADERS THAT POSITIVELY CHANGE YOUR CULTURE

FlexChip's engineering culture had to change or FlexChip would go under. Frank, vice president of engineering, was responsible for developing and implementing the ability to pass manufacturing seamlessly between plants in Germany, Vietnam, and the United States. At each plant, people spoke the local language and had a different culture. Frank's plan was to turn his individual contributor engineers from focused software development and process designers into transformational leaders, who could and would then lead the global cultural change.

Individual contributors (ICs) embody an organization's culture. They work in ways that are consistent with the real (though not always official) values of the organization. Through their attitudes and behaviors, organizations can change their cultures to significantly improve morale and productivity. ICs can and should be a primary force for cultural change and performance improvement.

ICs are generally not thought of as leaders because they do not sit high on the organizational chart. However, their in-depth experience with the real work of an organization gives them the insight and opportunity to identify and lead significant innovations. Great ICs lead, not through formal authority, but through being highly respected for their expertise, graciousness, and teamwork. ICs influence entire organizations with minimal formal support and recognition; they are the foundation of a culture of greatness. Affirmative IC Leadership programs quickly transition ICs from being isolated individuals, working independently, to a rich, highly influential resource.

In this chapter, you will learn how IC leadership can drive significant performance improvements and cultural change. The chapter shows how two organizations used Affirmative Leadership to transform ICs from isolated individuals to organizational leaders. DigiAd was trying to create a seamless customer-centric culture. FlexChip was creating a new engineering culture to drive a significant change in manufacturing facilities in different parts of the world.

DIGIAD—CREATING A COMPREHENSIVE CUSTOMER-CENTRIC CULTURE

DigiAd was a seller of yellow page advertising space that was transitioning to offering integrated print and digital advertising solutions. While the STL program discussed in Chapter 10 led to great sales team leadership, the DigiAd executive team recognized that their sales and service people needed to adopt completely new attitudes and behaviors as well. Five hundred sales representatives needed to transition from a "commodity sell" to a more complex and subtle selling process that focused on establishing an emotional connection. Similarly, the eighty customer service representatives in the DigiAd in-bound call center needed to transition from dealing with very high volumes of relatively simple print advertising issues, (for example, a wrong phone number in an ad in the phone book), to handling complex questions about "click" traffic profiles, slow website response times, lost page connections, billing complaints, and many other issues. All DigiAd personnel interacting with DigiAd's customers were expected to embrace the same customer-centric values and be able to execute the business processes that make customer centricity a reality.

DIGIAD DISCOVERY

Identifying the stars for DigiAd's programs was relatively straightforward. The stars were highly respected sales and customer service representatives who had demonstrated a passion for the customer centricity program and at least some success either selling to or servicing the more complex digital solutions. The sales program drew from the ten national regions, the service program from the Ohio sale center.

The Discovery Workshops followed the standard process. As the DigiAd exemplars worked on defining their Purpose statement, there were excellent discussions about the importance of passionate commitment to customer centricity, in-depth knowledge of the digital offerings, and the skills of closing sales or resolving customers' issues. Table 11-1 shows excerpts from the DigiAd Purpose statements.

DigiAd Sales Representatives	DigiAd Service Representatives
I am passionate about being a customer-centric account manager. As a trusted advisor with uncompromising belief in our solutions, I provide tailored solutions that generate abundant leads and superior return on investment.	I am a customer champion. I am positive, knowledgeable, and an effective communicator, empathizing with and owning any customer situation. I am empowered to provide balanced solutions that cultivate customer confidence that lead to retention of customers and lasting great relationships.

TABLE 11-1. DigiAd IC Purpose statements.

Although these are separate groups, they, along with the STL objectives described in Chapter 10, align around core values that are the foundation for a culture of great customer centricity.

Feeling great about the definition of their objectives, the groups moved on to define their Big Steps, excerpts of which are shown in Table 11-2.

Here too, cultural alignment is apparent. The Big Steps are the path to mastery for DigiAd's customer-centric culture.

Each of these Big Steps was further defined by Principles and Learning Tasks. The Learning Tasks were practical leadership development exercises. The participants did tangible work on developing trusting relationships and leading others. Now when clients interact with virtually anyone at DigiAd, they see the same culture, values, and commitment to customer centricity. When these types of IC Affirmative Leadership best practices are defined for many interrelated roles, or even just a few key IC roles, and later adopted by thousands of ICs, there is a strong likelihood of creating a culture of greatness. Few organizations would expect ICs to assume so much leadership of a cultural change.

LAUNCH

The key challenge of the DigiAd sales program Launch Workshops was the sheer number of 450 Sales Representatives (SRs) to coach in a very compressed time—three months. These 450 AMs were scattered in more than 40 areas, including Kona in the Hawaiian Islands; Anchorage, Alaska; Dry Lake, Nevada; Chillicothe, Ohio; Dothan, Alabama; and Newburg, New York. The speed of the deployment and geographical dispersion required DigiAd to use people who worked on Affirmative Leadership programs full-time as the facilitators of the AM Launch Workshops.

The Launch Workshops themselves were extremely success-

	DigiAd Sales	DigiAd Service
#1	OWNERSHIP: I am accountable for my own success. I treat being an account manager as if it were my own business.	CUSTOMER CENTRICITY CHAMPION: I will be the one to make it right! I own the customer situation and see it through to resolution.
#2	ACCOUNT PRIORITIZATION: I am extremely efficient at identifying and prioritizing the opportunities in my market in order to optimize my daily sales productivity.	EFFECTIVE COMMUNICATOR: I connect with my customer on a personal level by actively listening, empathizing, and asking questions to fully understand their issues.
#3	SOLUTION KNOWLEDGE: My knowledge and understanding of our print and digital products enables me to provide valuable, tailored solutions for my clients.	ADVANCED KNOWLEDGE: I utilize my in-depth knowledge of products, processes, systems, and other departments to make effective decisions.
#4	RELATIONSHIP BUILDING: I connect with my clients, serving as a trusted advisor to develop long-term relationships.	TEAM PLAYER: I positively collaborate with internal/external partners to quickly and effectively resolve customer situations.
#5	SALES EXECUTION: My passion and persistence make me an effective account manager.	BALANCED SOLUTIONS: I collaboratively pursue every means possible to make good on our original promise, while balancing with the financial interest of the company.

TABLE 11-2.   DigiAd IC Big Steps.

ful because they led to very deep discussions and increased understanding of the sales and service roles. For example, as Bonnie, who had an on-call service team, said: *"We did more team building and more to ramp up the new people in six hours of this program than we had accomplished in the previous three months of trying."* And as Alfredo, a new salesperson who sells primarily to Spanish language customers, put it: *"This was fun. I learned so much about our philosophy, products, and techniques in this session. I just can't wait for the weekly exercises."*

THE MOMENT OF TRANSITION

There is a point in all IC programs when learners convert from being tactical, transactional ICs to becoming Affirmative Leaders. They go from being driven by events and circumstances around them to synthesizing and balancing multiple conflicting factors. They find a clear direction, and then drive events to achieve a desired result. This conversion often seems sudden but is actually the culmination of all previous work. It is a magical moment when someone realizes she can be a leader, knows how to lead, and sees immense value in making a leadership contribution to those around her.

For most of the DigiAd salespeople this transformational moment came during the fourth Big Step, "Relationship Building." After systematically working on developing a strong mental model of customer centricity and learning how to prioritize accounts and understanding the scope and power of the integrated print and digital solutions, the DigiAd salespeople turned their attention to emotionally connecting with customers. The Learning Tasks, such as aligning with executives and building trust, stressed listening to the real desires and needs of the client, articulating what they heard back to the customer, and tying it to the DigiAd solution. As people focused on making a real connection, there was a jump to a new consciousness and everything came together. As Troy, a salesperson in North Carolina, recorded as part of his reflection (referring to a visit with a kitchen remodeler):

"I asked Jim (the kitchen remodeler) what he thought was most important for a customer to know about his service. He reached

for a book of pictures of kitchens he had remodeled and talked with considerable excitement about how each of his clients just loved their new kitchen and often said 'it was a dream come true' for them.

"At that moment, I just knew what would transform Jim and how DigiAd would help make it happen. I realized that Jim was really in the house dream business and that he shouldn't have a quarter-page ad about home remodeling but instead a video on a website where Jim and some of his clients could talk about creating/having their dream kitchen.

"I fed this idea back to Jim telling him that I thought he was really a dream maker, and he swelled with excitement and pride. I also told him that I thought that print ads just weren't going to capture his energy, and would he be open to having DigiAd video him and having the video, along with video of some of his clients and their kitchens, on a DigiAd-designed and -hosted website. He almost jumped out of his chair he was so excited.

"Knowing that Jim was ready to purchase the complete pack-age, I called our tech support person and put him directly on the phone with Jim to discuss the video and the website. Jim got even more excited. Then I told him that I thought we should also redirect his current print ad, so I called the CSR handling his print ads and we pulled the current ad back, set up a process for doing a redesign, and processed the order for the entire print and digital ad on the spot."

All the elements of being a great Affirmative Leader as a salesperson converged in this Big Step. The sales reps brought a strong internal model of customer centricity to their meetings and a deep understanding of potential solutions. They listened to clients' real value messages, which enabled them to make an emotional connection and influence the direction of the discussion. They found the best solution and presented it in a compelling way. As the key connection between the client and DigiAd, these salespeople created a profound vision of success, influenced the client to see the greater opportunity, and led a team that produced a win-win result.

DigiAd's service reps tended to transition to affirmative leaders near the end of the fifth Big Step, "Balanced Solutions," often while they were on the phone with a customer. As Leila put it:

"I was working with a customer who was really upset. Her website had been down for twenty-four hours during the holiday season and this was causing her to lose a lot of sales. I knew that I needed to make her feel heard and at the same time get the problem solved. I stayed very present with her, restating her fears about the lost business back to her and telling her the actions I was taking as we were speaking to fix the situation.

"I contacted the tech escalation specialist using IM and briefed him on the situation. We decided that he needed to join the call so I conferenced him in. He asked her some questions and said he needed to reset the site and could she wait a few minutes while he did the reset and checked it. She said 'yes.' He reset the site in about three minutes.

"She was still upset about the lost business so I asked her what would satisfy her and she said a month's credit would do. I knew this was at the edge of my limit, but this was a situation that we had screwed up so I told her we could do that. She thanked me profusely. It was really cool to handle all of this—her anger, the technical problem, the financial problem—all at once. It was amazing how it feels when it all comes together."

For most of the DigiAd service reps, Affirmative Leadership came as a feeling of complete mastery of very complex and demanding situations, often with considerable emotional and financial implications. They were, as one CSR put it, *"the center of the universe"* and had a great sense of their own importance, influence, and power. They thought of themselves as leaders representing the best of DigiAd and being the best people possible.

As a result, DigiAd has a seamless, highly integrated customer-centric culture. Everyone who regularly interacts with customers shares the same passion. Everyone knows how to efficiently follow a customer-centric business process. This true, functioning, customer centric culture is the realization of the CEO's dream.

FLEXCHIP–CREATING A NEW GLOBAL MANUFACTURING CULTURE

FlexChip had been a leading manufacturer of high volumes of a single, general-use microprocessor that were used primarily in servers, desktop computers, and laptops. However, this market had stagnated and much of the growth in the microprocessor industry was in mobile devices such as data phones and tablets that required significantly different business and manufacturing processes. FlexChip's survival depended on its ability to change the engineering culture in its German facility quickly and completely enough to drive changes into its recently acquired German, Vietnamese, and American manufacturing plants, each of which spoke a different primary language, had different business processes, and had values specific to their countries.

One group, Manufacturing Engineering (ME), had the potential to span all three facilities and unify the company. ME was responsible for the design of production flow, the automation of the manufacturing lines, particularly software tools, and fixing specific production glitches such as quality problems with a specific machine. However, ME had been centered in the German factory for years prior to the consolidation of the company and had narrowed its focus to a limited number of transactional functions, primarily fixing short-term software problems for the German production line.

FlexChip management decided that ME was best situated to drive the transformation to an integrated, multi-facility high mix/high volume business culture. This transition would require thirty software and production design engineers to change from the German facility's focused technocrats to transformational, global business process leaders. As Frank, the head of PPT, put it: *"My engineers are incredibly resistant to change. They are East German purist engineers and are among the most closed and inflexible people in the word."* FlexChip believed that if they didn't completely change the company in a year, they would be completely out of business.

FLEXCHIP DISCOVERY

FlexChip had a significant challenge in identifying its stars because the change they required was outside everyone's prior experience and they were under extreme time pressure. The Discovery session had to be at the German facility because the bulk of engineers were based there, and the German team was seen as the likely leader of the global change. Klaus, the German ME manager, only learned about the one-day Discovery Workshop seventy-two hours before we arrived and sent out e-mails to potential stars just forty-eight hours before the program was to begin. He didn't explain much—he just asked them to clear their schedules for the day.

To make matters even more challenging, the German engineers selected to participate in the Discovery Workshop had never been told about the change in expectations for their role. Frank, therefore, started the workshop with a two-hour presentation about the roles ME and the engineers would play in the global change. After many questions and some clear discomfort, the group got to work on defining their purpose for a role that was literally brand new to them. Fortunately, defining an "objective statement" (which was a better word than "purpose" for these engineers) was consistent with their engineering notion of solving problems, so initial resistance faded quickly. Table 11-3 shows the Purpose statement from the FlexChip ME engineer program.

The FlexChip Purpose statement was challenging to create because it was the first time the new ME engineer role was being specifically defined. Not surprisingly, there was impassioned debate about the overall intent of the role and language of the objective. For example, one of the most contentious but culturally important discussions was about the words "driving" and "multi-fab." These ME engineers had been in a reactive role for years, simply responding to requests from the German production managers. Now, Frank was expecting them to become leaders driving change across all three manufacturing facilities. Wolfgang, one of the star engineers, argued that Frank's perspective was *"unrealistic, would not be supported by production management and wasn't something any ME engineer would want or be able to do."* Wolfgang's remarks were typical of the resistance to change in the company's engineering culture.

Hans, on the other hand, argued strongly, and ultimately persuasively, that like it or not, FlexChip had to change and that production management was so swamped that only ME could lead the change. While everyone acknowledged that

---

FlexChip ME Engineers

I thrive on conceptualizing and driving innovative, scalable solutions that bring sustained, competitive advantage to multi-fab manufacturing. I inspire collaboration that leads to flawless, timely delivery of significant value for customers, enabling mastery of today's and tomorrow's challenges.

TABLE 11-3. FlexChip Purpose statement.

this was going to be incredibly difficult, in the end everyone agreed that developing and leading these complex solutions was the right direction for ME. Acceptance of the new role by the stars, the first step in converting the ME and then the FlexChip culture, had been achieved.

Once the FlexChip stars generally accepted the idea that they had to be transformational, in the terms defined in the first part of the Purpose statement, they began to look at the bigger picture of the leadership requirement. They realized that FlexChip's customers and the industry at large did not understand the new business model that FlexChip was trying to implement. In particular, the new business model required more collaboration between the customers and Flex-Chip to define specific products and ramp up manufacturing than was the industry norm. The star engineers realized that they needed to become spokespeople for FlexChip, speaking directly to customers and through industry forums about the value and sophistication of the FlexChip process. It was a very ambitious goal that supported Frank's strategy, but was seen by everyone as incredibly difficult to achieve. As Marlene, one of the ME managers said: *"I like the direction, but it is very scary too."* The FlexChip ICs had now advanced to defining their role as changing whole global industries.

While there was a general feeling of being nervous about the scope of the new role, the stars plunged on to define their Big Steps. Table 11-4 shows excerpts from what they produced.

This is an extremely demanding program. It affirms ME's controversial new role, solidifies technical fundamentals, and then radically changes the ME engineering paradigm in ways that will also change the FlexChip culture. And all this was to be implemented in an environment that did not like change!

The star Principles were equally innovative and demanding. Table 11-5 shows excerpts from their "Innovation Leadership" Big Step.

FlexChip Affirmative Leadership engineering Principles

FlexChip ME Engineer
#1   ME VISION: I embrace the ME role as the "innovation engine" of the FlexChip value chain.
#2   GREAT FUNDAMENTALS: My deep domain expertise (for example, yield, logistics, and software development) maximizes my impact.
#3   DELIVER VALUE: I identify immediate high-value opportunities.
#4   BREAKTHROUGH SOLUTIONS: I lead idea generation and the evaluation of new concepts.
#5   INNOVATION LEADERSHIP: I work with others to establish new global standards and methodologies that will expand FlexChip's competitive advantage.

TABLE 11-4:   ME engineer Big Steps.

FlexChip ME Engineer	
Big Step	**INNOVATION LEADERSHIP**
Principles	• I am continuously learning about FlexChip's business needs and the surrounding ecosystem. I use this knowledge to anticipate market trends, understand opportunities to increase profitability, and market the resulting need for change.
	• I actively manage, utilize, and enhance the company's intellectual property portfolio. Intellectual property is an important part of FlexChip's competitiveness, and it is much easier to expand strategic partnerships with an appropriate intellectual property portfolio.
	• I lead and support global standardization efforts and the development of new methodologies to increase efficiency, allow reusability and cross-fab transferability of solutions. The result is to allow standards to create a more scalable solution and the foundation for innovation.

TABLE 11-5.   ME engineer Principles.

set a clear expectation that these formerly German-focused engineers are now expected to learn to influence an entire industry.

Developing the initial Learning Tasks into a formal program was particularly challenging. Because of limitations on travel expenses, we could only visit Germany once, so after the Discovery, some German stars worked intensely with us to create a complete program. We completed the learning tasks in less than twelve hours and used them in the Launch Workshop the next morning (Table 11-6).

These Learning Tasks drove ME engineers out of their comfort zones into IC best practices and led directly to extraordinary leadership at FlexChip and even to industry transformation.

LAUNCH

FlexChip's Launch Workshop was the most challenging we encountered anywhere, because of the culture. Specifically, there was a very big difference between the engineers raised in communist East Germany with its history of repression and the engineers who had been raised in a liberal democracy. The older engineers were very hesitant to talk openly.

Frank began by discussing why FlexChip had to evolve in the market and the role of ME in leading the transformation. While everyone had heard this before, now they had to do something about it and they weren't happy. But we plunged ahead anyway and began the process of Read/Discuss/ Praise/Anchor for the ME engineer purpose statement. The Learning Groups with the younger engineers immediately began intense, spirited, and positive discussions about the change in role.

Heinrich, one of the older engineers, refused to participate in Read/Discuss/Praise/Anchor. He said it was too much like the indoctrination process used by the East German com-

FlexChip ME Engineer	
Big Step	**INNOVATION LEADERSHIP**
Learning Tasks	• Interview FlexChip executives or managers from different functions (for example, marketing or sales) about the view of the future trends in the market. List three learnings and determine the implications for ME engineers. If immediately available, attend a quarterly communications meeting. Share with my team. • Identify a source of industry information outside of FlexChip (for example, a website, forum, conference, and Frank's e-mails). Review one item from this source every week for one month. List three things learned and determine the implication for ME engineers. Share with my team. • Interview someone from a partner organization (for example, a customer, or vendor) about their view of future industry trends. List three things learned and determine the implication for ME engineers. Share with my team. • Identify a company in a different industry that has a function similar to ME. Visit the company and benchmark their processes. Integrate learning with the ME plan. • Identify one opportunity or forum to influence a standards discussion. Create a strategy for developing greater influence. Share with my manager.

TABLE 11-6. ME engineer Learning Tasks.

munist and Nazi dictatorships. He said that, in communist youth camps, children were indoctrinated in loyalty to the state by being forced to read pledges of loyalty to the government, discuss them in politically correct terms, and write their own versions of them. If they did not make their support for the state clear enough, they were penalized severely—even, sometimes, with imprisonment and death. So Heinrich and several other older engineers in the session overtly rebelled against the Affirmative Leadership process.

Marlene, who was coaching most of the older engineers, tried to address their concerns by referring to the source of the content—their peers—and explaining that they were all expected and encouraged to change the content to make it work for them. She emphasized that there wasn't a specific correct answer, and that they were to use the star foundation to design their own program. She made it clear that MEs needed to move into more of a leadership role. In response to this last comment, Frederich, also one of the older engineers, said: *"I have been a database expert for thirty years, and I am really good at designing and developing databases. I don't want to lead anyone."* Heinrich's resistance to change seemed to be shared by the other older engineers.

While some of the resistance was clearly due to the East German cultural issues, the group also seemed to resist Marlene's leadership because she was a younger female (she was the only female engineer in ME). After an intense discussion, Ulf, who seemed to be the real informal leader of Marlene's team, simply asked Heinrich and Frederich to give it a try. Because this came from Ulf, Heinrich and Frederich agreed to try and the discussion about the Purpose continued. A tremendously challenging barrier to a cultural change had been temporarily overcome.

After this, the FlexChip Launch Workshop settled down and ran mostly normally. The groups with engineers under thirty-five years old, coached by Dietrich and Rolf, really thrived. The only consistent issue that came up was skepticism that production management would be open to the new ME role, to which Frank said: *"Part of my job was to ensure that the new ME engineer is well received."* In the evaluation at the end of the Launch Workshop, the members of Dietrich's and Rolf's groups were very positive, and Marlene's group indicated that the process was acceptable. Affirmative Leadership at FlexChip had launched.

In debriefing the session with the coaches, Rolf said: *"When the wall came down, one of the things that we in East Germany realized is that we had forgotten how to talk. I loved this process, and I think my team loved this process because this gives us a very safe, very systematic opportunity to talk, or at least learn to talk. But Heinrich, Frederich, and some others haven't learned to talk yet and it scares them to be expected to talk. A lot of the reaction was their not knowing how or not wanting to talk."*

Marlene jumped in and added a comment about Frederich and his desire not to be a leader. She said: *"Not only is there resistance among the older people to talking, they have learned that leadership, particularly leadership that goes against an established authority, can be very dangerous. In the GDR* (German Democratic Republic—aka East Germany), *if you spoke out and were a leader, you could be shot . . . and that is not a metaphor."* It is certainly understandable how this type of background would create great initial resistance to a neuroscience-based learning process and to any form of leadership program that created perceived risk for the learner. The ME Affirmative Leadership program was working as designed for everyone under thirty-five, but it was going to be shaky for everyone over forty-five. This program would need special support. The cultural context really mattered.

THE MOMENT OF TRANSITION

The FlexChip ME engineers had multiple moments of significant transition during the third Big Step, "Deliver Value," again during the fourth Big Step, "Breakthrough Solutions," and building up to the fifth Big Step, "Innovative Solutions." These represented specific stages of development that transformed the ME culture and, as a result, began to transform FlexChip. For example, in the third transition, the ME engineer candidates exerted leadership that drove the definition of global manufacturing standards and built credibility for FlexChip's innovative approach to manufacturing. Hans summarized the transition by describing his experience presenting a paper at an international manufacturing conference in the United Kingdom. Here are his recorded learnings:

"I had never been to a conference like this before. There were 6,000 people here and everyone seemed to know a lot about manufacturing. I was in a medium-size room for my presentation, which was just fine with me, and too my surprise it was filled. I realized that the issue of high mix/high volume was critical to almost all mobile devices—particularly data phones—and the people really wanted to hear what I had to say. I made the point that the switch from high mix/low volume had to start with people's images of themselves as much as of their business. If they kept thinking of themselves as specialists in the old way, then nothing could change. Only after getting people to reinvent themselves was it possible to redesign the manufacturing process and systems.

"I got lots of questions about how we changed people and in particular about the connection between sales and the manufacturing systems. I told them that part of our training was to think about the entire picture and this helped, because in high mix/high volume the customer had to be more closely integrated with manufacturing decisions.

"They seemed to like the presentation. I got a good ovation after the talk and about ten people came up to me to talk with me about my ideas. I felt like I have influenced some people. It was scary, but the experience was really great."

There is an obvious progression in the development of the FlexChip ME's leadership. They began the process as a narrowly focused support group for German manufacturing and ended by influencing the industry.

RESULTS

The measurable results, where available, support the impact of IC Affirmative Leadership on the productivity and culture of the organization. For example, the DigiAd Sales Representative certification program reported that 98 percent of the sales reps displayed the desired customer-centric attitudes and behaviors (the remaining 2 percent left the company). This translated into a doubling of the sales of digital products. By the end of the Affirmative Leadership program, the DigiAd executives knew that 100 percent of their salespeople had the same attitudes and behaviors as their top performers.

The DigiAd CSRs had both a similar certification program and specific outcome measures. Because several less effective people had been screened out during the program, the certification rate was 99 percent. More importantly, the outcome measures were very strong. First call resolution doubled and problem escalations dropped from eighty-four per day to only fourteen per day by the end of the program. This was achieved without a significant increase in time on a call. Being great customer-centric Affirmative Leader CSRs directly impacted transactional performance metrics.

FlexChip had a more problematic situation. Near the end of the program, FlexChip was purchased by another company, and all of the management team was let go including Frank and the German fabrication managers. The sudden change in ownership overshadowed the ME program. While there were some anecdotal indicators of success prior to the ownership change (for example, Dietrich said that he saw a real difference in how people were interacting with production, and Elsa, the plant manager, said she saw that ME's presentation had become much more strategic and persuasive), no systematic information was collected. It appeared to us that there was a significant change in the engineers, and Frank told us that he thought the program worked, but there wasn't a final result.

CONCLUSION

Commonalities are apparent across these IC programs. All of the ICs went through three levels of realization. They realized they could be leaders. They realized they knew how to lead. They realized that being a leader created immense value for themselves, their organizations, and society. These three realizations meant that they were Affirmative Leaders who had the motivation and ability to create cultures of greatness.

From the organization's perspective, IC Affirmative Leaders bring more energy and direction to organizations, and because there tends to be many ICs, the organization has more energy and direction, and the culture of the organization and surrounding society improves. These ICs changed from isolated individuals performing conscribed functions to transformational leaders of the organization changing their cultures in ways that increased productivity and made them great places to work.

LIVING IN A CULTURE OF GREATNESS

REAPING THE REWARDS OF A LEADERSHIP-RICH ENVIRONMENT

At Lots-of-Parts, a large auto parts chain, Affirmative Leadership–led stores outperformed comparison stores by 5.25 percent in sales and 30 percent in loss management.

At MegaChip, Affirmative Leader customer service personnel were twice as accurate at forecasting client demand as comparison groups, with each point of improvement in forecast accuracy increasing profits by $50 million.

At PropInsurance, a large property and casualty insurance company, Affirmative Leadership–led agencies grew policy count by 15 percent as compared to a corporate average of just 2.9 percent.

Leadership is ultimately about producing results, and these are just some of the many examples of how Affirmative Leadership changed organizations. As one vice president of operations described his Affirmative Leadership culture, *"The focus, the teamwork, the energy, the results . . . it is unlike anything I experienced before. It is magical."*

This chapter shows what has been and can be achieved in an Affirmative Leadership culture. It then suggests an idealistic, but possible, future for organizations and, ultimately, our society.

AN EXEMPLARY CULTURE

After our work with QuickBurger, we asked Kevin, the project manager, to describe the Affirmative Leadership process and its impact on their culture. We were preparing for a presentation to the CEO of the largest home improvement chain about Affirmative Leadership and thought that getting a client's language might help the presentation. Kevin is a hard-nosed, analytic businessperson, not given to being effusive. He paused for a few seconds, frowned, and then said: *"Tell him it is magic, just plain magic!"*

Others have made similar statements about both the Affirmative Leadership process and the results it produces for their organizations. Speaking about the overall Affirmative Leadership process, Steven, a director of leadership development for a major defense contractor, said, *"Affirmative Leadership is like a great magic trick. You enjoy watching, get excited about what you saw, but do not have a clue as to how it occurred. The magical part was completely hidden, but it was a great experience."* He went on: *"People eventually came to accept Affirmative Leadership because it produced results that mattered."*

Similarly, Sarah, the director of leadership development at a major retailer, compared Affirmative Leadership to the introduction of the kitchen microwave. This is how she described her Affirmative Leadership experience:

"Affirmative Leadership is like the microwave. Prior to the microwave the primary paradigms for heating food were on a stove or in an oven. It took a while and the container got very hot. People wondered how it was possible to put food in a box, push a few buttons, and seconds later take out hot food in a cool container. For most people, it was just magic. But over time, people learned that it worked every time and weren't concerned about how it worked. Eventually, Affirmative Leadership will

be like the microwave; accepted because it always produces results, even if only a few people understand how it works."

People talk this way about the process because the results grow from a gradual accumulation of subtle, interrelated influences. Many are invisible to the learners or coaches. The whole is far greater than the sum of its parts and results in completely new behaviors and attitudes.

For example, respect and Fair Process pervade everything in the program. Respect is inherent in everything from the invitation letter to the stars to the Wisdom Discovery Workshop, the group creation of the wisdom during workshop, the language used to introduce the coaches to Leading Group Learning, the development of self-directed learning through adaptation of the learning tasks, the expectation of contribution to the weekly meeting, and the final closure workshop.

Similarly, Purpose, Mastery, and reflective learning are overtly and covertly everywhere. All three are explicitly used in the Wisdom Discovery, Leading Group Learning coach training, and Launch Workshop. For example, they are present in the phrase, "it is important because . . ." used in anchoring the Big Steps and Principles and the transition between Big Steps, where the edits in the Launch Workshop are reviewed and tied to the Principles and Learning Tasks. Both explicitly and implicitly, Fair Process, Purpose, Mastery, and reflective learning, and the motivation and meaning they provide, are continuously reinforced. In hundreds of small ways, Affirmative Leadership subtly creates a culture of greatness.

The effects continue and grow throughout the program. The facilitator guiding the Leading Group Learning uses Affirmative Leadership to guide the potential coaches into being Affirmative Leaders. In turn, the coaches are models for Affirmative Leadership for their Learning Groups. The other participants, bathed in an environment of Affirmative Leadership, transform into autonomous Affirmative Leaders as they progress from the more basic levels of the early Big Steps to the more sophisticated leadership capabilities of the later ones. This culminates in the closure review with the recognition by individuals and their coaches that a transformation has occurred.

Overall, virtually every component of Affirmative Leadership, even very small components like specific terminology and the facilitator's posture, integrate and combine to generate neural responses and influence development. Even the management tracking system is positive and support-oriented without sacrificing the structure of clear and specific performance expectations. Participants are not sure why or how they have changed so much, but they know that they are better people and employees after the program.

As Melia, one of the participants in the CompTech Transformational Leadership program, stated:

> *"I initially thought this was just another task list, and the last thing I needed in the world were more tasks. Then I realized that the tasks, group discussions, and my recorded learnings were guiding me to think about my current job differently. Then I realized that I was starting to do the job differently. Then I realized that I was actually doing a significantly different, more exciting, and really more important job than I had been doing previously. I changed from being very tactical to a strategic leader and didn't even know I was changing. It was all very mysterious but incredibly exciting."*

Affirmative Leadership programs immerse participants in a new way of learning and leading that gradually, seamlessly, and very naturally becomes a new way of being.

Not surprisingly, the new self-perception driven by Affirmative Leadership changes people's perspective of the opportunities in their company. Through Affirmative Leadership, people see new opportunities for growth, development, and influence. For instance, Greg, one of the first-line managers at LocalPower, said:

> *"I was ready to leave this position. I felt like there was no way I could win. Management was always micromanaging me, and the union reps always seemed to be fighting me. It just wasn't very much fun, and I was about ready to give up and move on. But during this program, I started to be able to manage up better and was able to actually influence some of the personnel policies, and it took a lot of work, but I got the relationship with the union guys turned around, particularly about working toward a greater purpose. I see lots of ways I can develop more in this job. And I like it a lot better."*

Through Affirmative Leadership, a dissatisfied and potentially disruptive employee became a positive leader, improving his own job satisfaction and impact, his team's morale and productivity, and his overall contribution to the success of the organization."

When organizations implement one Affirmative Leadership program, the role that is the focus of that program influences others to become more positive and purpose-driven. When executives, first-line managers, and individual contributors are all Affirmative Leaders, the organization's culture changes and productivity soars. Everyone makes a major leadership contribution to the organization, and the organization becomes purpose-driven, productive, and a good place to work.

When multiple roles in an organization go through Affirmative Leadership programs, the culture itself changes in many important ways. Fair Process becomes a deep cultural value. Everyone treats everyone else with great respect, giving people and the culture itself honor and dignity. The respect comes easily because everyone is aligned on a core Purpose. People are good at their roles because they have worked hard to achieve Mastery. Everyone knows that everyone else is deeply committed to achieving a greater good and has the attitudes, knowledge, and skills to make a significant contribution to achieving that greater good. As such, everyone is a leader wherever they are on the organization chart. Executives, middle managers, team and departmental leaders, and a wide variety of individual contributors contribute to leading the organization, and they do it almost unconsciously. These organizations are great places to work.

Affirmative Leaders understand that they exist in a larger social context and act to build Affirmative Leadership capabilities in other organizations and more generally in society. Most Affirmative Leadership programs include some element of social consciousness or participation in events and organizations outside the organization. A software quality assurance program, for instance, included a Learning Task that focused on joining and consciously contributing to a global quality forum. Even more telling was a program at Comptech, an international computer giant, that offered an Affirmative Leadership program to their suppliers because it made the suppliers more productive and easier to work with, and thus, better partners. Some of the suppliers declined to participate and soon lost out to those who did because the non-participants were more expensive and generated more challenges. Comptech, for its own direct benefit, set out to create an Affirmative Leadership ecosystem.

The idea of creating an Affirmative Leadership ecosystem brings us to our deep Purpose. We want to make the world a better, more productive, and happier place. We know this is a grand statement, but why shoot for anything less? We didn't set out to change the world, just to improve leadership in a few organizations, but we stumbled onto something bigger. When we first told a colleague about the possibility that Affirmative Leadership could actually make for a better society, he cautioned us to hide this perspective because no one would believe us and it would discredit our work, which is why we saved this grand vision for the end of the last chapter. But perhaps, just perhaps, after you go through all of the nitty-gritty details and science of how to develop and implement an Affirmative Leadership program, you can see how this can be effective for one role in an organization, then several roles, then the organization as a whole, and then the related ecosystem. It is not a huge leap to see how ecosystems could link together to change society for the better. Creating a culture of greatness anywhere in the world is both achievable and desirable.

THE BOTTOM LINE

While all of this talk of cultures is nice, the bottom line is, of course, the bottom line. Quantitative proofs matter. The first level of quantitative proof is the results of the certification programs. The certification programs measure a "demonstration of capability" of the attitudes and behaviors of the stars; that is, they measure each person against the very best people in that role.

Thousands of participants have been through Affirmative Leadership certification programs. More than 90 percent of them have been formally evaluated and objectively determined to be showing the same attitudes and behaviors as the best. The numbers show conclusively that the retained learning from Affirmative Leadership is well beyond any traditional methodology.

Not surprisingly, raising everyone to the same levels as the stars consistently produces excellent financial performance. The numbers at the beginning of this chapter are numbers any organization would love to have. However, there are skeptics. A vice president of a flooring chain said: *"Are you telling me that you can achieve something in a matter of weeks and months that I have not been able to achieve in years?"* The leadership teams in all of these organizations and many others would all say: *"Yes, Affirmative Leadership consistently produces these extraordinary results."* When asked the follow-up question, *"How does it do it?,"* the best they can say is what Kevin said: *"It is magic, just plain magic!"*

We say the Affirmative Leadership approach efficiently and with surprisingly little effort from participants creates a culture in which every person aspires to and achieves greatness. Everyone becomes as good as the very best. When everyone in an organization becomes an Affirmative Leader, the synergy and energy create an extraordinarily exciting and productive culture of greatness.

ACKNOWLEDGMENTS

Writing a book is always a team effort. We want to thank the many people who helped us develop the methodology and supported us during the development and writing process. We apologize if we missed anyone.

There were many people who helped us develop the Affirmative Leadership methodology presented in this book. In many instances, they helped us by forcing us to examine new ideas and processes, which was often uncomfortable, but always valuable. Their tremendous support, both emotionally and financially, during the many years of development is greatly appreciated. Our thanks go to Aleemna Wray, Bryon Bailey, Dale Lockwood, David Hooten, Derek Glos, Doug Crane, Heather Ziegler, Jeff Adams, Jaime Hegeman, Jason Choy, Jocelyn Burgess, John Bernard, Jon Revelos, Joseph Friedman, Karen Ness, Kathryn Tecosky, Leah Alibozek, Mike McCauley, Nathan Johnson, Peter Galen, Prashant Bhat, Regina Williams, Shelley Todd, Steve Benson, and Tammy Nakao.

Getting a book written and published requires lots of teamwork and contributions too. Our thanks go to Christina Parisi, our editor at AMACOM books, and the entire AMACOM team for seeing the potential in our work and guiding us through the publication process. Special thanks to Mike Snell, our agent, for seeing the potential in our ideas long before they became a book and to Libby Koponen, our development editor. Libby was fanatical about making sure the book was well written, which helped us write a much better book.

Thanks to the Cerebyte team who kept the business going while we were writing the book. Larry Rebich and Ryan McCauley made sure that our persuasive technology was the best in the market and always ran smoothly. Eileen Galen, Amy Dunn, and Ryan Dunn are our marketing arm, and they are doing great publicity to make the book visible to all of its many potential readers. Tim Kerrigan is responsible for our business development. He kept leads flowing even though we were often too focused on the book to provide much sales support.

Finally, thanks to our families. Our kids and their spouses were just great in supporting our efforts. Andrew, David, Hannah, James, Jill, Julia, Kristen, Lia, Mark, Rory, and Scott are all tremendous. We are so proud of them and thankful for their support. Our wives—Debbie and Elizabeth—are amazing. They supported us through the emotional hills and valleys of writing a book and tolerated the many hours the book required. We love them dearly.

INDEX